What people are saying about …

THE TRUTH ABOUT LIES

"Life comes down to moments. And not all moments are created equal. Some matter *a lot* more than others. In those crucial, axis-point moments, the kind that set the trajectory for our future, how will we respond? Will we succeed or fail miserably? Will we keep our footing or fall on our faces? How do we navigate the moments of life with wisdom beyond our years and face the temptations of our hearts with courage and resolve? In *The Truth about Lies*, Tim leads us into a new place as he sets a new framework for how to live and how to live well. If you're ready to take the journey, I can't think of a better guide."

John Mark Comer, pastor of teaching and vision for
Bridgetown: A Jesus Church, and author of *Loveology*

"Tim Chaddick has the ability to strip away the impenetrable exoskeleton of a thing and crack it wide open, exposing its beating and sometimes damaged heart. He writes with graceful accessibility but also careful urgency—a combination that is all at once refreshing and convincing."

Marielle Wakim, *Los Angeles Times*

"Tim is a leader we should pay attention to. This book is about the testing of a leader—something we all struggle with. Tim provides practical perspective and helpful application for the moments when our mettle is tested and our character revealed.

You'll gain crucial insight into the process of maturing as a follower of Jesus, the blocking and tackling of temptation and pushing through, the constant daily renewing of our minds and hearts. It's messy, but meaningful. It's raw, but refined. If you are a leader, read this book!"

Brad Lomenick, author of *The Catalyst Leader* and *H3 Leadership,* former president and key visionary of Catalyst

"Tim is one of the new generation's preacher/teacher/writers who I'm thankful for. He's passionate, clear thinking, articulate, deeply rooted in Scripture, and in tune with culture. The depth, transparency, and simplicity of his writing make this book both engaging and helpful. I'm certain you will be blessed and benefit greatly from it."

Brian Brodersen, pastor of Calvary Chapel, Costa Mesa

"Tim Chaddick is such a gift to our generation. He combines theological expertise, pastoral concern, and cultural sensitivity in a way that few people are able to do. His gifts culminate in this book to take on a topic we need to look at with fresh eyes—the topic of temptation. The claim of the book: If we know how to approach it, temptation can form in us Christlike character. Read this book with a highlighter!"

David Lomas, pastor of Reality San Francisco and author of *The Truest Thing about You*

"Tim Chaddick has given us a gift with *The Truth about Lies*. In the middle of our temptation, God is doing a great work in us. This book is biblical, wise, and necessary."

Philip Nation, director of Content Development, LifeWay Christian Resources, Teaching Pastor, The Fellowship, Nashville, Tennesse

"Tim has done a brilliant job helping us think wisely about temptation and understanding it, and therefore we can respond to it with God's help before it wrecks us. If you have ever been tempted or ever think you will be, this book will help you live more closely to the ways of Jesus."

Tom Hughes, lead pastor of Christian Assembly Church, Los Angeles

"Tim Chaddick is a man of profound Scripture-formed insight and wisdom. His life and words draw me deeper into the presence and joy of Christ every time we are together and when I read his works. In *The Truth about Lies*, Tim leads us on a discovery of truth that helps deliver us from lesser things and brings us into a fuller, faithful experience with Jesus. I am so thankful for this book and this man; you will be well pastored as you read *The Truth about Lies*."

Britt Merrick, founder of The Reality Family of Churches and pastor at Reality Carpinteria

"Tim Chaddick is able to communicate to a post-Christian audience as well as anyone I know. In this book, he skillfully shows how the narrative of our culture and the questions it raises can only be satisfactorily answered by the narrative of the truth of the gospel."

Rankin Wilbourne, senior pastor of
Pacific Crossroads Church, Los Angeles

"In *The Truth about Lies*, Tim Chaddick shows that temptation is not an obstacle to following Jesus; it is an opportunity to become like Jesus. In a book that will be relevant until sin is silenced and the Devil vanquished, Chaddick gives more than a strategy for battling temptation; he points to the Savior who gives us the power to overcome it. I'm incredibly thankful for Tim Chaddick and his courage to remind us all that if we have heard the truth from heaven, we can face the lies of hell."

Jeremy Treat, PhD, pastor at Reality LA, adjunct
professor of theology at Biola University, and
award-winning author of *The Crucified King*

the TRUTH
about LIES

TIM CHADDICK

the TRUTH
about LIES

THE UNLIKELY ROLE OF TEMPTATION
IN WHO YOU WILL BECOME

David C Cook®

transforming lives together

THE TRUTH ABOUT LIES
Published by David C Cook
4050 Lee Vance View
Colorado Springs, CO 80918 U.S.A.

David C Cook Distribution Canada
55 Woodslee Avenue, Paris, Ontario, Canada N3L 3E5

David C Cook U.K., Kingsway Communications
Eastbourne, East Sussex BN23 6NT, England

The graphic circle C logo is a registered trademark of David C Cook.

The website addresses recommended throughout this book are offered as a
resource to you. These websites are not intended in any way to be or imply an
endorsement on the part of David C Cook, nor do we vouch for their content.

All Scripture quotations are taken from the Holy Bible, English Standard
Version® (ESV®), copyright © 2001 by Crossway, a publishing ministry
of Good News Publishers. Used by permission. All rights reserved.
The author has added italics to Scripture quotations for emphasis.

LCCN 2014959541
ISBN 978-1-4347-0524-2
eISBN 978-1-4347-0937-0

Published in association with the literary agency of
D.C. Jacobson & Associates LLC, an Author Management Company
www.dcjacobson.com

The Team: Andrew Stoddard, Andrew Meisenheimer, Amy
Konyndyk, Nick Lee, Helen Macdonald, Karen Athen
Cover Design: Heather Wetherington

Printed in the United States of America
First Edition 2015

1 2 3 4 5 6 7 8 9 10

052915

CONTENTS

chapter one

THE TROUBLE WITH TEMPTATION

I can resist everything except temptation.

Oscar Wilde

If the heroic tales from the maritime tradition of bravery and sacrifice at sea have a lasting legacy in our culture, it's this—the captain goes down with the ship.

This is why we react so strongly when that doesn't happen. Two recent incidents remind us that some captains abandon their posts, leaving the bravery up to the passengers. First was Captain Francesco Schettino of the capsized *Costa Concordia* off the coast of Italy in 2012; the second was Captain Lee Joon-seok of the *MV Sewol* in South Korea in 2014. The photographs are all over the Internet— the haunting image of Captain Lee stepping to safety while leaving hundreds in danger aboard the sinking ferry. Once ashore, he was immediately arrested.

Yet there were other crew members, including twenty-two-year-old Park Ji-young, who stayed, safely evacuating as many as possible from the ship. Running from floor to floor of the vessel, she summoned the crew to help in whatever way they could to save passengers and put their safety first. She even gave up her own life jacket.[1]

Why do we admire this young woman? Why do we use a word such as "hero" when we speak of her? Most likely it's because her conduct displayed *conviction*. We have a sense of "rightness" about her actions, that she did what *ought* to be done in such a moment of need and crisis. We applaud it.

Conversely, we feel a tinge of fear when we hear about the captain, because all of us know perfectly well that there are times when we know what we ought to do but don't do it. As we read the evening news, learning the details of a tragic story, we tell ourselves that whatever it takes, we want to be ready when life puts us to the test. We understand that the choices we make in this moment affect the next.

But getting to the place of abandoning ship or saving lives is not just about one isolated choice or event—it's the culmination of our choices throughout life. The sinking ship crisis did not *create* convictions; it *revealed* them.

We want to be prepared. Tests and temptations will come. The preparation and power we need for them is what this book is about.

Defining moments never stand alone. Yes, they make the headlines, provide plenty of conversation pieces, and serve as inspiring stories or cautionary tales. But defining moments are always preceded by countless others. The big decisions we must make in public, in the spotlight, are influenced by the daily, character-shaping choices made in private.

Often referred to as *virtue*, this habit-forming strength of character[2] is essential for how we face all the obstacles and opportunities of life. In answer to three great questions about life, C. S. Lewis used the image of a fleet of ships setting out to sea.[3] *Mission* is where you are headed, *ethics* is making sure you don't bump into the other ships, and *virtue* is making sure your ship doesn't sink. The glorious truth of the Christian gospel is that we are provided not only with a new direction and destination but also with the incredible power and conviction to make it there. The gospel teaches us how to stay afloat.

It also has the power to rescue sunken ships.

Conviction is a certainty about what to stand for. Many, and not just religious people, admire it. The London-based writer and well-known atheist Alain de Botton was visiting the Metropolitan Museum of Art in New York City when he came across a painting that struck him so much that he bought the postcard of the famous painting in the museum shop, just so he could look at it again and again on his flight home.

The painting was of the great philosopher Socrates, who was condemned to death in the city of Athens for his belief in philosophy—he refused to worship the city gods. In the painting, Socrates is lying there on a bed, all his friends weeping because he's about to be executed, and he is holding a deadly cup of hemlock that will send him to the grave. With a bold hand raised in the air, knowing his fate, he drinks to his death.

"If the postcard struck me so forcefully," Alain said on his way back to London, "it was perhaps because the behaviour it depicted contrasted so sharply with my own. In conversations, my priority was to be liked, rather than to speak the truth.… But the philosopher had not buckled before unpopularity and the condemnation of the state.

He had not retracted his thoughts because others had complained. Moreover, his confidence had sprung from a more profound source than hot-headedness or bull-like courage."[4] Alain's realization at the Met is crucial: temptation reveals our deepest convictions.

Or, to put it more Christian-ly, temptation reveals our deepest loves.

You and I may never captain a ship or be held on trial or be forced to drink poison because of our beliefs, but we are all responsible for our lives and will face tests. They may not always be huge or dramatic—in fact, most of them will be somewhat small and much more subtle—but we will face them nonetheless. How we choose to handle these tests reveals what matters most. And over time, it shapes who we will become.

Whenever I read in the news a story of moral failure among leadership, scandal within an organization, or infidelity in a marriage, I experience this two-part reaction. Part of me wants to say with a surge of confidence, "I would never, ever, do such a thing." I may even want to give myself a pat on the back, reminding myself of all the ways I have shown courage and integrity in the past, how much Scripture I have memorized, and how many church activities I've been involved in. I feel that I am safe because I'm clearly not a candidate for such a downfall. I've got this.

On the other hand, part of me trembles. I am reminded of how fragile humanity is, and how I am, in fact, a fellow human being, and like it or not, humans have a very long track record of making bad choices. And I begin to think of my mistakes in the past, and I slowly spiral downward, concluding that because I am vulnerable, defeat is inevitable.

That all might sound a bit dramatic (and I must confess I can be a bit dramatic), but it actually reflects two very common responses I see in the church regarding the reality of temptation. Faced with the possibility of making bad choices, we often respond either by lifting ourselves up, assuming that it would *never* happen, or by beating ourselves up, assuming we can *never* change. Denial or despair.

The trouble is, neither response can truly help us face real temptation.

DENIAL DOESN'T WORK

Seven years after planting the church I pastor, I was given my first sabbatical. Three months off from regular leadership responsibilities to refresh and recharge for the next season of ministry. My leadership team thought this would be a good season for me to take a break. Since the birth of the church, my own family had grown—from one daughter to three. No boys, only girls. Needless to say, there are a lot of tears in my house (and that's just me!). I was looking forward to nothing but family adventures and reading deep theology. I didn't realize that God was going to take me deep into my own soul.

Accepting the challenge of a dear friend, I decided that I would not read as many books as I could, which, he reminded me, can sometimes be another way I distract myself from the deeper issues in my heart. I would keep it simple—read Scripture, work through one book on spiritual disciplines, and journal my progress. No big deal.

And at first, it wasn't.

Until I got to the theme of self-examination.

Ugh.

I preach on this topic frequently. I teach how Scripture tells us to examine ourselves and why it's an essential part of our growth. But with busy schedules, demanding workloads, and community needs, it's often the first thing to go.

It happens with pastors too. The unexamined drives and motives operating in our hearts don't just go away or disappear in our busyness, however. In fact, they shape our choices and behavior *within* the busyness.

It was with this in mind that I began to put my pen to paper and write down both the strengths I had observed in my life as well as the weaknesses. We all know our shortcomings are harder to write about. The so-called "big sins" in our lives are fairly obvious, especially to those around us. My wife, dear friends, and fellow leaders would be the first to point them out to me, if I asked. But while reflecting on my weaknesses, I slowly became aware of the more subtle aspects of my fallen nature, the ones that lie deep beneath the surface. We all know that you could be a regular churchgoer, tithe-giver, prayer-say-er who doesn't "drink some or chew or go with those that do" and still be giving in to great temptation.

What surprised me, however, was not that I discovered fallen motives within my heart; it was my unwillingness to acknowledge them.

One morning, convicted of a specific case of envy and jealousy, I wrote in my journal: "Lord, please heal me of —"

And I stopped right there. I didn't want to write it down. If I wrote it down, then I was admitting to myself its reality in my heart.

Wait a minute … why did I stop? What was I doing—cheating at Solitaire? Why was it so hard just to write down this particular attitude in my heart? Maybe because it was easier for me to deny it than to face it head-on. This is a classic example of the heart's ability to cherry-pick what it wants to see and what it does not. Denial might give off an appearance of power, but, really, it is just weakness masquerading as strength. It's giving in to self-deception.

In 1 Samuel 13–15, we read of a great king, Saul—Israel's first. His debut is solid. He is praised by the masses for a great military victory in the first few years of his career. He is good-looking and God-fearing. Yet over the course of his life, he becomes paranoid, jealous, and even crazy violent. A long personal and national decline was followed by a crushing defeat at the hands of the opposing Philistine army, leading Saul to fall on his own sword at the end of a brutal battle. The end of his story is tragic. Now, looking at a person like Saul, it's easy to say, "No way. Not me."

But that's what everyone says.

When I was fourteen and one of my classmates, frustrated with my teenage ego, called me conceited, I roared, "NO I'M NOT!" Then I proceeded to look for a dictionary because I actually had no idea what the word *conceited* meant. (It means you are full of yourself, for anyone who wants to know.) But learning to admit pride takes more than looking up the definition in a dictionary. On the outside, sure, my decisions may look vastly different from another person's, like Saul's. But on the inside, the Bible tells us that we all share this ability to deceive ourselves. It's pretty simple, actually—humans have been practicing it forever.

When Saul is confronted by the prophet Samuel for disobeying God, he practices what some call "perspective switching." He does not want to admit that he is susceptible to such temptation. So he dismisses an unfavorable view (Samuel's) for a more favorable one (his own).

Haven't we all done this? A friend calls us out on something we have done wrong, and it hurts our ego a bit. So we call on our *other* friends for a second opinion until we find one we like. Saul does not receive correction; he defends his position. He chooses to believe a lie rather than the truth. His unwillingness to admit his weaknesses became a pattern in his life that was destructive, to himself and to others. When you read in the Old Testament about the big, defining moments in his life, you quickly realize that they were preceded by many other moments. They shaped the type of king he would become.

How many of us respond to conviction in the same way Saul did? Perhaps more of us than we are willing to admit. It can even spread to entire groups of people, creating a type of congratulatory support group for those who assume they are above the rest. Like Saul, we have this inner lawyer waiting to defend us when confronted by areas of weakness. In those moments, a miniature trial takes place within ourselves and we rarely lose a case.

But the more we give in to denial, the further away we move from reality and the easier it becomes to cross boundaries. Self-justification is like a gateway drug to a world of bad choices.

In contrast, there is the way of honesty and openness, knowing that God does not reveal our weaknesses to harm us but to heal us.

My hesitancy to get real and raw before God that day during my journal writing was simply driven by a desire to keep up an appearance, to "lift myself up." But I was soon reminded that's the worst thing I could do. God already sees my weakness anyway—there was no use in pretending. And His conviction is an invitation to live out of our true selves, who we really are before God through Christ. It's a life that moves beyond mere appearance to substance. Because of what the Bible says about the pervasiveness of sin in the heart, lifting yourself up as the solution to overcoming temptation doesn't work. It's only giving in to a different temptation.

But the next option is equally ineffective.

DESPAIR DOESN'T WORK

When approaching the end of my sabbatical and taking stock of all the great times my family had experienced together, I made a significant discovery about myself. Reflecting on what God had revealed to my heart over the summer, I decided to write it all down in two simple categories: strengths and weaknesses. On one side of a page, I wrote down all the strengths present in my life, and on the other side, the weaknesses.

To be honest, I was a bit surprised when the list was completed. Most of my strengths were connected to my gifts—abilities that God has given me to help other people, to teach, and so on. But my weaknesses, I noticed, were mostly character issues—bad attitudes and behaviors that remained unaddressed. While the big temptations had always been on my radar, I realized I was giving in to smaller ones.

I took this list to my wife, to whom I have been married for fourteen years, and said, "You know me better than anyone. Are these observations true?" And to top it all off, she said, in the most gentle, kind, and truthful way, "Yes, yes they are."

Now, I'd love to say that I handled this feedback in a wonderfully mature Christian way, but I didn't. I sulked. Outwardly, I'm sure I looked calm and contemplative, but on the inside I was throwing a bit of a tantrum, not unlike my toddler might.

Why do I even bother? I thought.

There is just no hope for my maturity.

I need to inflict some kind of pain and punishment on myself for my lack of growth.

If the first approach toward our inclination to temptation is to bury it, the next is about staring at it and beating ourselves up. This response is so pervasive that if we speak with people today who have no particular religious background about Christianity, many might assume that we basically live lives of self-torture. Some might even believe that wallowing in despair will somehow purge and cleanse us of our sins and our proneness to give in to temptation. It's true, of course, that before we can receive and appreciate the solution for our souls, we must first understand that our souls are actually in great need. We must realize that we are spiritually bankrupt before we can experience the riches of salvation. But to think that beating ourselves up for our fallen condition actually accomplishes something is a concept completely foreign to the Bible.

Another king in the Bible will help here. As he looked at all his achievements, success, and splendor, the ancient Babylonian king Nebuchadnezzar bragged to himself about his glory and power, as though he were a god. We are told in Daniel 4 that a judgment sentence was immediately given from heaven against his pride—he would lose his royal authority and be driven from Babylon into the wilderness.

The portrait given next of the king is pretty freaky. We're told he lived like a beast of the field, eating grass like an ox, and growing out his nails like bird's claws. He had lifted himself up, and now he had been brought low. He was in despair. Humbled by this experience, he eventually would lift his eyes to heaven and praise God and honor Him for who He is, and God would restore him. But here is the point: the humbling experience by itself did not restore him; *it was the recognition of his need for God and turning to God* that brought restoration. It would have accomplished nothing for him to continue roaming as though living in the wild, with clawlike fingernails and crazy long hair. This would not transform his character.

It's not the humbling wilderness that can rescue us; it's where we learn to look in the wilderness that can rescue us.

In the New Testament, the apostle Paul makes a fascinating distinction between godly sorrow and worldly sorrow. There is a kind of grief over our brokenness that can lead to repentance and a kind that doesn't. "For godly grief produces a repentance that leads to salvation without regret, whereas worldly grief produces death" (2 Cor. 7:10).

Grief over human brokenness *by itself* doesn't bring change. When I give in to temptation, I may be grieved, but why? Perhaps I am grieved simply because people have seen my mistakes. Worldly sorrow is that which grieves the loss of worldly approval.

But, on the other hand, if I've realized that my wrongs are because I have turned from God, then my grieving is the loss of the only approval that really matters—the approval of God. Then this humbling moment can cause me, as it did with King Nebuchadnezzar, to turn my eyes toward heaven and open my heart to what only God supplies. Despairing over my character flaws and beating myself up over them doesn't change me. But if these moments prod a turn toward heaven, then I can find true strength and authenticity.

GETTING TO THE HEART

My summer sabbatical taught me that I'd approached temptation and character growth with a self-centered confidence. When I'd experienced some kind of success in these areas, I had congratulated myself, thinking how I was just crushing it in my spiritual life. But when I'd experienced failure, giving in to temptation, I had become paranoid and paralyzed, thinking that there must be no way out.

But if one thing is clear when it comes to temptation, it's that "God … will also provide the way of escape" (1 Cor. 10:13). I was just trying the wrong door.

It's not merely enough to memorize a couple of general principles about being courageous in the face of temptation. It's allowing God's spirit to change us from the inside out, day by day, turning us into the kind of people who live out of brand-new identities, not founded upon our own work but upon God's. The conviction and confidence we need to sail in the direction of a future hope comes not by looking in toward ourselves but in looking up toward heaven.

With self-centered confidence, success will make you prideful and failure will make you fearful.

But God-confidence will make you faithful.

Temptation has a revealing effect, uncovering the heart's desires, proving both the *depth* and *direction* of your conviction. It shows what you're really committed to, what you really care about, and what has captured your deepest affections. The type of people we become—courageous, fearful, paranoid, brave, stingy, generous—is shaped by what we love the most. The trouble is, according to the Bible, our loves are all out of order. Will I be willing to admit a wrongdoing when I am convicted by God's Spirit, or will I choose to bury it because I love appearing faultless in front of people? Will I be willing to admit my need for correction, or will I choose a facade because I love appearing right before others? Will I say no when I am asked to work overtime, or will I say yes because I love to be needed? The greatest temptations lure us by replacing truth with lies, authenticity with appearance, and love of God with love of self.

We must look within and ask, what is it that we love most?

Like it or not, these choices must be made daily. And our choices have consequences, affecting not only our own souls but the souls of those around us, for good or bad. But this reality should neither lead us to denial nor leave us in despair. Because the topic of temptation raises the issues of the heart, it's not enough to have some good principles in place, hoping that through our rule keeping or image management we will actually bring inside-out change. Temptation is a battle that's not about winning or losing; it's about discovering who you really are. And what you love most. This book is about how the gospel transforms us so that even moments of temptation become the training ground for a life of abundance, as our hearts are radically reshaped and reordered by the love of Jesus.

Because ultimately, the key to facing temptation is not a principle; it's a Person.

chapter two

AN EDUCATION IN GRACE

For the grace of God has appeared, bringing salvation for all people, training us to renounce ungodliness and worldly passions, and to live self-controlled, upright, and godly lives in the present age, waiting for our blessed hope, the appearing of the glory of our great God and Savior Jesus Christ.

Titus 2:11–13

As a teenager, not only was I into the typical teenage angst and the behavior that came with it, but I was *proud of it*. However, when I began to realize that maybe failing junior college due to wild behavior and bad relationships wasn't actually that awesome, I knew I had to make some changes.

So I tried desperately to become a "good person." I cut down my substance abuse to two nights a week instead of five, actually tried to keep a job, and became vaguely interested in religion. But instead, I was slowly becoming angry and depressed. Something had to change. I had to change.

My strategy was simple: focus on the badness of what I did, in hopes that I might develop a distaste for wrongdoing and all manner of vice. But it wasn't working. When I experienced any amount of progress, I became arrogant, wondering why my other friends weren't advancing as I was. Or, when I relapsed into my old ways, I became angry with myself. How could I actually *change* my desires? Outwardly I looked fine. People would compliment me for trying hard. But it was a lie. Inwardly I was a mess.

It was then that I discovered the true power for change. I finally accepted an invitation from an annoying Christian who kept bugging me to come with her and her friends to an "evangelism" event south of San Francisco, promising "great" music, free food, and T-shirt giveaways.

Oh dear. What was I doing?

Well, whatever it was, I was compelled to go. I had to. Though I had been drinking heavily the night before, not falling asleep until 4 a.m., I got the reminder call at 8 a.m. and somehow felt as if I had slept all night.

When I pulled up to the event, I couldn't help wondering if I had just made the worst decision ever. But it was there, in the midst of cheesy music and a stage performance drama that would make you wince, that I met Jesus.

The message was simple, clear, and piercing. I saw Christ in all His truth and beauty; His life, death, and resurrection; and the life that He wanted for me. I was so full of joy that I actually decided to sleep in the church gym because I didn't want to leave. I was changed. And not just for a day. Months went by and I felt that I was both instantly changed and constantly changing. I was still facing old struggles, but it was all different from before. I was discovering one of the most transformative aspects of God's grace in the heart—old affections being overpowered by new affections.[1]

EDUCATING THE HEART

I think I have one of the best jobs in the world. As a pastor, I get to tell people about the beauty of Jesus, how He has changed my life, and how He can change theirs. And not only do I get to talk about this, but I get to watch it happen.

However, it's not always nice and neat. Sometimes it looks pretty messy. Before this change happens, the situation is often dark and bleak. People who are aware of their need for change often realize the need to deal with sinful patterns but don't feel they have the power to do it.

I think of the man in my church who is trapped in drug addictions and struggling to see change, thinking that it's enough to just go to church and follow some rules and guidelines. Or the woman who served in our church all the time but had no joy and was almost always irritated, complaining constantly about other people. I think of entire groups of people who once experienced great enthusiasm but who are now plateaued in a state of dry and lifeless patterns.

Is there hope for them and for us? Of course, the answer is yes. *But how does this change happen?*

It's a statement often attributed to Aristotle that "educating the mind without educating the heart is no education at all." The idea is that we are creatures of desire, of motivation. Behind every "what" we do, there is a "why"—something driving our decisions. When we seek to learn something, such as a subject in college or how to drive, we learn for a purpose. The human heart does not only seek instruction, but it operates on incentive.

The default approach to change seems to be this: a constant barrage of "CHANGE CHANGE CHANGE CHANGE CHANGE." If I can tell someone one hundred times a day that he or she should stop lying/cheating/hurting/manipulating, then eventually that person's will can be shaped in new directions. Right? I certainly heard this advice in my social circles growing up. I even hear it among some Christian circles today.

The problem is, it doesn't work.

When it comes to temptation, we can't think that the whole moment is won or lost depending on how much we see our need to change. We also need to know *what* needs to change and *why* it matters. We must know what actually reshapes and redirects our desires toward the path of life. Well, that is one of the beautiful truths of the Christian faith—we are told what needs to change *and* we are given the power to change.

What our hearts need is an education in *grace*.

When C. S. Lewis was asked what the difference was between Christianity and all other religions, he replied, "Oh, that's easy. It's grace!" Indeed, there are roughly 4,200 religions in the world, according to some estimations,[2] and the difference between Christianity and all the rest could be summarized in that one little word.

When Paul wrote a letter to Titus, a leader in the early church, he told him that the problems Titus faced in the culture and the church were fundamentally problems of the heart. Like us, Titus encountered the same issues as we do today—plateaued, defeated, dry, and discouraged believers feeling trapped by the lies of sin.

Paul's letter reminded Titus that he should not give up, because overcoming temptation is possible as our hearts are trained and educated in a living relationship with God Himself, by grace.

So what exactly is it about grace that teaches us and changes us?

GRACE REDEEMS YOUR PAST

I'm not sure what comes to mind when you think about your past, but when I think about mine before I met Jesus, it was like this giant burden that I carried on my shoulders. It weighed me down. It left me longing for deliverance. People in every century and cultural background have experienced this pain or shame over what they have done or what has been done to them, wondering if there is healing at all or if we are just doomed to collapse under its weight.

The people of the first century, in the apostle Paul's day, longed for the same freedom, only they hoped it would somehow come from the many gods of Greco-Roman society. The idea was that you might be able to find deliverance from the sorrow, pain, and burden of the past by showing yourself worthy to the gods. If you did, maybe, just maybe, the gods would show up. They called this an "epiphany," an appearance of deliverance. Everyone was waiting for it, hoping it would happen someday. Paul's response to the desire of this culture is classic and controversial:

That epiphany you want? It's already happened.

Earth-shattering events have taken place, there has been an unveiling, an appearing of God's grace to lost people—grace that delivers us from the domain of darkness and opens up the prison doors for those in captivity.

Now, saying that God's grace appeared does not mean that God's grace was somehow absent beforehand. It's not as if God was supergrumpy for thousands of years but all of a sudden had a good morning, drank some coffee, and decided to become gracious.

No, Paul is saying that the grace of God, *already existing*, has become publicly available to all, for in the Person of Jesus Christ, the grace of God is shown. Jesus Christ is the ultimate grace of God. His appearing was not for a select few but for everyone, *without discrimination*. His life, death, and resurrection have brought what all of us need.

Through Him we receive *complete* forgiveness.

If you're a Christian, you know this, but do we always live like it? We easily fall into the temptation of thinking that our sins are only partially forgiven, as if God has given us only some kind of cosmic–kick-starter program in which He donates 60 percent toward the cause of our forgiveness but we have to take care of the rest on our own.

But this is a total contradiction of the gospel.

The truth is that the moment we believe, the second we confess, we are completely forgiven.

I know a man in my church who seemed to live a tormented life. He went about serving on Sundays and involving himself in community life as though he had a death sentence hanging over his head. In response to a troubled email he sent me one night, I did what I often do when I get troubling emails—I called him.

As we spoke, I quickly picked up on several statements indicating that he simply didn't feel forgiven of sin. I asked him, "Do you not know that you are forgiven?" He said, "Oh, I know that in my distant past I am forgiven, but as for my recent past, I should know better, and so I am riddled with guilt."

I asked him to show me in the Bible where a distinction was made between distant sins and recent sins, but he couldn't provide me with a reference.

That's because it's not there.

Many of us stumble in this same way, thinking that we are only partially forgiven. That night, I simply told him this: "If you don't think that recent sins can be forgiven, then you are saying that the cross of Jesus Christ is not enough to forgive sin at all."

After a moment of silence, he agreed with a sigh of relief.

Here is why this is so important for facing temptation and becoming the people that God wants us to be. Paul goes on to say in his letter to Titus that we must renounce sin. But you can only *renounce* what you know is forgiven—both the sin of your past and the sin you've yet to commit. Grace isn't just about the sin you've already committed. You are forgiven right now in the present moment.

GRACE TRANSFORMS YOUR PRESENT

I was speaking on the topic of temptation at a retreat. After one of my sessions, a man in his midforties approached me with his head hanging down. He told me that he had been divorced recently because an eight-year-long affair he had with another woman had finally come to light and destroyed the marriage. But even after such devastating consequences, he still could not resist affairs with women. He felt trapped, he confessed. "I don't know how to say no," he said.

Though his situation may be drastically different from the temptations you face, we often find ourselves in the same position. We just don't know how to say no. The drive for what is forbidden just seems to be too strong.

In conversations like this, the most common question I get is, "What do I do with my desires?" After all, we are taught in culture to simply *express* them. If we desire it, we're told, then go for it.

But stop and think about this for a moment.

Aren't there are all *kinds* of desires in our hearts?

Yes, there are—even competing and conflicting desires. Which ones should we express? Which ones should we indulge? I'll be honest, the other week I really wanted to cut off the car that wouldn't let me in the lane as I got on the 101 freeway in Hollywood; should I have expressed this desire because it was *there*?

The more I think about it, the more I realize that this view is largely driven by emotion and intuition alone. But Scripture is very clear—there is right and there is wrong, there are things that glorify God, and there are things that grieve Him. There is truth and there are lies. Just because we have an appetite for something doesn't automatically mean we should indulge in it.

Paul says in Titus 2 that we are to say no to ungodliness and worldly passions, referring to lust, unrighteous anger, selfish ambition, and other desires like them. While many of us know this, we become frustrated because we have tried to say no many times and yet see little change. What should we do? Pay closer attention to the fine print of the apostle's epistle. Paul says we must be *trained* to renounce ungodliness and worldly passions.

What does he mean by this?

Why does he say we must be trained?

I believe he says this for two reasons. First, he wants us to understand that learning to say no to temptation is a process. This clashes a bit with many modern Christian expectations, mine included. I just want to get zapped in an instant. But instead, Paul describes a process, one in which we are educated in the school of grace. That's one reason. The second reason why Paul says that we must be trained is because there are all kinds of *wrong* reasons to say no.

The man I spoke with at the retreat knew full well that what he had done—and was doing—was absolutely wrong. He knew what he was doing. But it didn't seem that he really knew *why* he kept doing it. I asked, "Have you ever stopped and really looked into the reason you say yes to every sexual encounter?" He replied with a simple "Not really." After an hour of more conversation and a time of prayer, we discovered together that affection and attention from women was how he felt good about himself, and how he received the validation he thought he needed. The light began to go on for him not only when this truth started becoming clear, but more than that, when he started to see that the true validation and affection he needed comes only from God through Christ. That night this man said he realized that he had been blind not only to the seriousness of sin (oh, it's not that bad, is it?) but also to the beauty of Christ (is it really that great?).

So often when dealing with the *what* of sin, we don't deal with the *why* of sin, the motive and drive behind the behavior. Add to that, we quickly forget the real power for change. The lies of sin blind us to the beauty of Christ. It's when we see both our sin for what it is and our Savior for who He is that we begin to experience radical change in the present.

Christ points us in a new direction, and He empowers us with new affections.

Thinking about motives changes the way we see temptation. Many of us only try to say no to sin because it might make us look bad or because we might be pushed out or shunned by friends or our circles of influence. But these incentives are focused entirely on ego. That is why they don't bring real change. Paul never appeals to self-focus when he talks about transformation. So how do we learn to live this new life and say no to sin and yes to righteousness?

By knowing that you are rescued from sin and death and loved with an everlasting love. This is what reshapes our motivation—it's the grace of God.

However, when it comes to grace, there are common misunderstandings. For example, some think that grace means "I can do whatever I want." But think about what this says. Suppose a wife says to her husband, "Even if you are unfaithful to me, I will never leave you" and the husband responds, "Great! Good to hear. I'm going to go have a couple of affairs this week, and I will see you when I'm all done!" Heartbreaking. If the husband really grasped the beauty of his wife's love and faithfulness, he should be led to be faithful. The same is true for the follower of Jesus. Why would we willingly embrace the very things that Christ died on the cross to forgive? If grace has touched your heart, you learn to say no to sinful passions. Grace is not a license to sin but a motivation to love.

To see change in our lives we must allow the gospel of grace to teach us. This happens as the Holy Spirit enters the inner dialogue of our hearts and reminds us of how the truth of Jesus bears on our decisions in that moment.

Distaste for sin is certainly a part of renouncing it. But that is not the whole picture. Your affections for what is wrong need replacing.

You need to love something else more.

Let's think of something less dramatic than infidelity in marriage and much more common to Christian experience: anger. Whether it's our short fuses, bitter outbursts, mean-spirited sarcasm, or passive-aggressive stonewalling, unrighteous anger is an issue for many of us. How does grace teach us in these instances?

In that moment of temptation, when something (or someone) has pushed our buttons, God's conviction raises a question that gets to the root of the issue:

Why am I angry?

It's a question we rarely stop to ask ourselves. Is it because perhaps we felt unvalued and unappreciated? The other week when one of my decisions was challenged and overturned at the office, I found myself becoming angry. Was it because I have a high need for control and I lost it in that moment? These questions help us to see what's really driving us. Conviction of sin takes place, and we begin to realize we should say no to this kind of anger.

But the process doesn't stop there. God reminds our hearts of the beauty of grace! The value we really need comes from God, and He is the One who is ultimately in control—not us. And that is a good thing. This is the better story that our hearts need in that moment of temptation, bringing healing to our anger. This leads to what Paul calls a "self-controlled, upright, and godly" life.

When I struggle with unrighteous anger, God convicts me of the wrongness of my attitude and then points me to the beauty of

Christ. Simply put, grace teaches us to say yes to what is right with the power of a new affection.

In mentioning these three categories of self-control, uprightness, and godliness in Titus 2, Paul is saying that change doesn't just happen in one part of your life; it happens in each and every part.

Grace is comprehensive.

First of all, grace changes the way you relate to yourself. You can find power for self-control as you recognize that fulfillment is found in glorifying God, not by gratifying your every whim.

Secondly, grace changes the way you relate to others. Because you have been accepted by God and have been given the glorious call and privilege of reflecting Him in the way you conduct yourself, you pursue an upright life—to be just, in the way that God is just, seeking the good of others around you because God has sought your good.

And thirdly, grace changes the way you relate to God. Knowing that God's favor toward you is undeserved yet lavishly given is the fuel your heart needs to run toward Him, not away from Him. Paul assumes that these wrong appetites won't just disappear, but that they will be overridden by a greater affection.

It's an incredible yet easily forgotten truth that grace empowers your growth! You don't pursue uprightness, godliness, and self-control in order to *earn* God's favor; you pursue these to *enjoy* God's favor. You aren't working to keep God around. Many of us operate in life out of the fear of losing something, and that is often reflected in the way we view God. "I've gotta do all this righteousness," we each tell ourselves, "or God will never come to me!" This is running on fear, not grace.

I have a beautiful three-year-old daughter, and she celebrates every time I come home from work. My two older daughters don't get that excited anymore, but this little one throws a miniparty. I love it. But recently, she has started to say something different when I walk through the door. With a cute high-pitched little voice, she says, "Daddy … you came back!" Came back? Of course I came back. Why wouldn't I come back? Did she think I was not going to come home or something? This is how we often feel about God. But Paul makes it clear you should be hard at work in the present, seeking growth in these areas of self-control, uprightness, and godliness, without fear of losing anything of ultimate value. God is with you and will come for you.

GRACE SECURES YOUR FUTURE

Recently, many young couples in my church have gotten engaged to be married; the ring has been given and a wedding date set. What you see during this engagement period is not dread (although wedding plans and in-laws have been known to drive couples crazy) but desire, a longing for that day to come. In a similar way, this is how we should live each day, with future hope giving us present power. We can bank on this because Christ has already given us His life, liberating us from the kingdom of darkness.

The ancient Greeks believed that there would be an end, an unveiling that would transform the world. Paul says God is the One who is going to make this happen. Grace gives you hope as you look ahead. Jesus has not only appeared in the past, but He will appear in the future and make all things new. This is called our "blessed hope." Christ will come and bring us to glory. Learning to live in light of this great fact should not bring anxiety; it should bring expectancy. And action.

To use a slightly modified classic saying, grace *has* delivered us from the penalty of sin, grace *is* delivering us from the power of sin, and grace *will* deliver us from the presence of sin. Why are we told this over and over again in the Scriptures? Because the power of Christian living is found in between the finished work of Christ in the past and the promise of His return in the future. We must hold these truths together in our hearts and minds if we are to overcome sin and temptation. But this is where we often slip.

If you are a music lover, then you know the pleasure of listening to your favorite album on headphones. I love hearing in both ears the sonic subtleties and nuances of great music and good production. If you love this experience, then you know how horrible it is when one of your earphones doesn't work. It drives me insane because I'm getting only half of the mix! You need both left and right ears to enjoy the music properly.

Like a pair of headphones, we need to hold both the truth of Christ's work in the past and the promise of His return in the future. But frankly, some of us are living with only one earphone in. On the one hand, you might be very aware of Christ's work in the past, but you have no expectation in the future, and so you are filled with worry and perhaps discouragement. On the other hand, you could be alert to the reality of Christ's soon return, yet be forgetting His finished work, and you end up being burdened with guilt, trying to work your way forward. You must hold both truths together.

You need to listen to grace in stereo.

Many of us give in to temptation because we are distracted by the "next big thing." You might be dissatisfied with your job or your current relationship or even your church. You might be tempted to think that the solution for your discontent is to find better versions of those things. To use the apostle's word, you are looking for an "epiphany," waiting for the next curtain to open on a stage for the thing you think will give you the hope you need—whether that be another career or another relationship. But if that hope is anything other than Jesus Christ, it's an illusion. It can never give you what your heart needs.

When we are distracted, giving in to the temptations of worldly passions, we find ourselves simply looking for recovery. But this is where grace educates our hearts. God is not in the recovery business; He is in the transformation business. The Scriptures tell us not only *how* to live but *why*, giving the incentive and motivation the heart needs to move forward and become who God wants us to be.

Grace brings about a change of mind *and* a change of heart and life.

You are not only *called* to grow, but you are *empowered* to grow. It does not happen by my own efforts of being a "good person," or focusing only on the badness of sin. Though legalism tries to capture the will, only grace captivates the heart.

If you were to say to a person behind bars in prison, "Be free!," it would be an insult. That is what religiosity and legalism does. But

… if the prison door has indeed been opened and a way of freedom made, then saying "Be free!" is not an insult but an invitation. Walk through the door. Jesus Himself has opened it.

Walking in this freedom and hope does not necessarily mean that old, sinful desires disappear immediately. But it does mean that they can be overridden by the power of new affections.

chapter three

WHO YOU WILL BECOME

*The most important thing about you is not the things that
you achieve; it is the person that you become.*

Dallas Willard

When most people think of the great king David, usually two names
come to mind: Goliath. And Bathsheba.

One story is about a moment of victory. The other, a moment of
defeat. In one we see faith and courage. The other, fear and cowardice.

Yet, what should be clear in our minds is that neither of these
are isolated incidents. And that is one of the reasons I think the
story of King David has captured the imagination of people for
centuries, because in studying his life, we are watching a process
take place.

Martin Luther King Jr. once said, "The ultimate measure of a
man is not where he stands in moments of comfort and convenience,
but where he stands at times of challenge and controversy." The way
we behave in a moment of challenge is never about one isolated
choice but a culmination of choices throughout daily life. Men or
women who have affairs, for example, relaxed the commitment to

their spouses a long time before, subtly yet effectively weakening the relationships before the fatal blow.

However, the reverse is also true. People who seek daily to love, honor, and serve their spouses, even in the mundane routines of life, are quietly but powerfully cementing their commitment. They experience incredible victories in life and marriage, even though they face hardships along the way. David certainly knew the power of small choices in his early life.

A PERSON-SHAPING PROCESS

The account is so famous that it has become the metaphor in culture for overcoming seemingly insurmountable odds. *New York Times* bestselling author Malcolm Gladwell needs to use only the two names David and Goliath in the title of his book and we all know that he will be telling us about underdogs, misfits, and the art of battling giants. Single-handedly, with faith in the great God of Israel, David brought down the massive Philistine opposer with one stone to the head.

What we must not forget, however, is that the David-and-Goliath moments are preceded by thousands of smaller but no less important choices.

I suppose every husband would say that he would take a bullet for his wife. But if I want to become that type of husband who would be able to make a giant sacrifice in a moment of crisis, I must be developing a lifestyle of self-sacrifice, including the small things such as doing whatever I can to relieve the burden of my wife's daily responsibilities. Even making the smallest of good decisions daily is like flexing a muscle that strengthens you for the challenges ahead. David knew how to flex this muscle.

It was in the isolation of his shepherding vocation at a young age that David could have given in to the temptation of brushing off his prayer life, ignoring his responsibility to protect the family flock, or stop practicing his aim with a sling.

But he didn't.

David was in a pattern of praise, prayer, and offering his abilities to God as He used them and guided them. David did the hard work necessary for his family business and protected the sheep under his care from danger. These were the days of obscurity, when his character was slowly being crafted. It was long before, armed with just a sling and five smooth stones, he would face a giant.

The courage publicly displayed on the battlefield is courage privately cultivated in the wilderness.

What we choose to do even in the small tests radically shapes what we will become and how we behave when the bigger trials come our way. Let's say you are a married man or woman and you encounter someone who you are attracted to. After some conversation, you discover there is strong chemistry between the two of you and it has become obviously clear that desire exists.

This is a moment of temptation.

What you decide is not only a matter of right and wrong, but it will demonstrate what, or who, is most valuable to you. Will you choose to confirm the lifelong commitment you have made to your spouse? Or will you fulfill the immediate longing you have to gain the momentary exhilaration that a romantic affair will give you? A decision must be made. It's a moment of testing. It does not create your convictions, but it does reveal them, displaying for all to see what matters most. David won his battle with Goliath and was eventually made king. But would he win the battle within himself?

What began for Israel's king as a lustful moment turned into an enormous sex-and-murder scandal involving the woman Bathsheba and her husband, Uriah. Yet in the whole story of David, we learn that long before his "big sin," there was another sin growing deep within his heart, beneath the surface and off the radar. It's not immediately apparent in the earlier chapters of his life, but the seeds of pride were taking root. These seeds of pride began to develop as patterns in his life—not listening to the voice of God, loving his position as king more than the purpose of a king, and manipulating people. He grew numb to conviction.

It was the root of pride that brought forth the bitter fruit of his other sins. C. S. Lewis's words are sobering on this point:

> According to Christian teachers, the essential vice, the utmost evil, is Pride. Unchastity, anger, greed, drunkenness, and all that, are mere fleabites in comparison: it was through Pride that the devil became the devil: Pride leads to every other vice: it is the complete anti-God state of mind.... it's Pride which has been the chief cause of misery in every nation and every family since the world began.[1]

Every choice matters.
Moments of temptation force us to make them.

We must move beyond viewing temptation as a series of isolated events to a person-shaping process.

UNTRIVIALIZING TEMPTATION

If you want to stick out like a sore thumb in Los Angeles, just read a Christian book in public. As a pastor who likes to read and enjoys caffeinating myself in the packed coffeehouses of the city, I get the strangest reactions when fellow coffee lovers glance at the cover of what I'm reading.

It was a perfect Southern California day, ideal for some great reading. My nose was in an old Christian classic when a gentleman across the patio of the coffee bar loudly (and awkwardly) said to me, "Hey, you know what the author Oscar Wilde said about temptation, right? The only way to get rid of temptation is to give in!" Thoroughly pleased with himself, he laughed out loud, folded up his *Los Angeles Times* newspaper, and walked away. Apparently, he saw the cover of my book—*Overcoming Sin and Temptation* by John Owen.

Why would anyone read such a thing? Why bother with something like the topic of temptation? Isn't that just for religious prudes and former addicts? This is probably why the man who saw my book laughed, but it also reflects a common attitude many of us have toward overcoming temptation.

In popular culture, temptation is often trivialized. It is used in advertisements for delectable sweet products described with diabolical words, as if Satan's entire agenda were simply to break our diets and give us diabetes. While temptation does take on greater meaning among Christians, it's easy to confine it to so-called capital *S* sins, such as alcohol abuse, extramarital affairs, and addiction to porn.

Now, these are awful sins, and temptation can most certainly lead there, but in reality, temptation is so much more, extending to the whole of life, even the most unexpected parts.

Why did we *really* serve at that last church event?

Why do we *really* want that higher position at work?

What were we *really* thinking when that lady stood in front of us at the grocery store with twenty items in the ten-items-or-less line?

In Los Angeles, Sunset Boulevard is known for being full of "big sins," making it difficult for a Christian to live there. Usually the imagination goes to that one section lined with strip joints, dive bars, and pot dispensaries. Places of temptation. But isn't the rest of Sunset Boulevard also filled with temptation? All twenty-two miles, from downtown to the coast, can lure you away with escapism, greed, materialism, religiosity, or injustice.

It doesn't really matter which block you are on.

In fact, if we understand temptation for what it is, it might be just as hard for a Christian to live in Des Moines, Iowa. Anywhere you live, there are ideas and opportunities that can lure you away from God. They just come in different packages. You could even be in the middle of nowhere and be tempted—Jesus was.

Knowing how He understood and faced temptation in the wilderness is essential learning for everyone seeking to follow Him. The journey is both challenging and encouraging, causing us to rethink the importance of daily decisions.

Because temptation can kill you or make you stronger.

I think it's fairly obvious to us that temptation can kill the soul. What is less apparent, however, is how it can become an opportunity for growth. Understanding this is a bit trickier to comprehend. But doing so can be life changing. The reasons we would miss this are if

- our view of temptation is too shallow, or
- our understanding of its role in our lives is too narrow.

If our view of temptation is too *shallow*, then we may be in denial, giving in to ways we are not even aware of, disintegrating our spiritual lives. On the other hand, if our understanding of temptation is too *narrow*, we despair, become discouraged and fearful, not knowing the power and purpose God gives us within it.

However, if we listen to what Scripture has to say on these issues, not only will we avoid a lot of pitfalls and pain, but we will also flourish in tremendous ways, understanding where our true identity lies and learning to live out of that with great hope and strength.

It's not a random fact that before Jesus entered into His public ministry as Messiah, He faced temptation in the wilderness. I think, at the very least, it shows us how necessary it is for every person to understand what temptation is and how we are to face it in daily life.

We can't afford to get it wrong.

And we also can't afford to miss out on the incredible growth that happens when we get it right.

The wilderness temptation was such an important event in the life of Jesus that it's recorded in three of the four gospel accounts.

In it are not the typical situations you would expect—in fact, on the surface, Satan's offers to Jesus don't seem to look all that bad.

Of course, that is where we would be wrong.

A LOOK BENEATH THE SURFACE

There is this crazy episode in chapter 8 of the book of Acts in which the apostle Peter rebuked a magician in the city of Samaria. The people in that city had been paying attention to this amazing magician until an evangelist named Philip came into town, preaching the gospel and performing signs by the power of the Spirit. As he did, many people believed, including Simon the magician.

However, after seeing the people of Samaria filled with the Spirit, Simon offered Peter money, hoping that somehow the apostle would "sell" the power of the Holy Spirit to him. This is when Peter got all spicy and called Simon on the carpet, saying, "May your silver perish with you, because you thought you could obtain the gift of God with money!" (v. 20).

What Peter went on to say revealed that Simon's main problem wasn't just that he was a sorcerer or a magician. Dealing with Simon wasn't a simple matter of burning his Harry Potter books and heavy metal albums; there was a deeper issue.

Peter called it out, saying, "Repent, therefore, of this wickedness of yours, and pray to the Lord that, if possible, the intent of your heart may be forgiven you. *For I see that you are in the gall of bitterness and in the bond of iniquity*" (vv. 22–23). What was really driving Simon? His desire to be great in the eyes of people. Magic served him well while the people thought he was great, but when the church came into town and people were converted, he joined the church as well.

But his heart still needed changing.

He was bitter because people didn't give him the praise they once did. Though the temptation on the surface may have for a time been sorcery, the hidden temptation was selfish ambition. His pursuit of the praise of men is what led him to become a bitter person in the bond of iniquity.

The pursuit of man's praise is, incidentally, what can drive many of our endeavors. People slowly become platforms, and our influence becomes our identities. It's a temptation in all our hearts, and it's chilling. Like Simon, a person can be driven by this hidden desire *before* their conversion, and even *after*. It just looks different on the surface.

In my younger years, my reckless behavior was interrupted when the tragic drug-induced death of a close friend shook me to the core. I started asking myself some serious questions: *Why can't I stop? Why do I, against all my good intentions, give in again? Can't I see the consequences?*

Though I didn't understand it at the time, my view of vice and temptation was too *shallow*. I was seeking to fight obvious sins such as sexual promiscuity and drunkenness, while being unaware of what was actually *driving* these sins underneath the surface.

For a short time my addiction to substances subsided, but that was only because I replaced them with a new addiction: a musical career. I was obsessive about it. I would lay awake at night, thinking, writing, and scheming. I even burned bridges with friends in order to advance my dreams, and I spent most of my money supporting my new addiction. I moved from using drugs to using friends.

On further reflection, I was so blind to the deeper temptations I was giving in to daily that I was letting them fuel the more obvious ones.

I didn't *ultimately* have an alcohol problem. I had a worship problem. When I dove into substances, I was looking for something to give me escape from pain. I didn't *ultimately* have a sexual problem. I had a worship problem. And I got into sinful and unhealthy relationships because I was driven by the need for validation. When I pursued what I thought to be a promising musical career, I was actually looking for something to give me salvation. I was building an identity on the influence I could gain through my talents. Beneath the surface I was giving in to the temptation to break the first commandment: have no other gods. My heart was enslaved to worshipping things other than God. Like Simon the magician, I was pursuing the praise of men.

We all have a "past," some skeletons in the closet, and those days might seem long gone. But it's possible that the same motives behind our bad behavior ten years ago lie behind our good behavior today. Even though the past seems distant, old motives can creep back in, all dressed up to go to church. I may not be getting wasted anymore (that usually doesn't go over well for pastors), but believe me, even Christian ministry can be driven, like Simon, by seeking the praise of men.

A BROADER PERSPECTIVE

Now, if we stop there, it might just make us superparanoid Christians and possibly leave us paralyzed in a state of constant fear, wondering which big trap lies around the corner. But there is much more to the picture. The second thing that can keep us from growth in the area of temptation is when our understanding of its role in our lives is too *narrow*. We need a greater understanding as to why God allows it in our lives.

God allows temptation.

That is a strange thought, isn't it?

The Bible is clear, however, that God Himself does not tempt us. God is not evil. As we shall see … He is not playing some cruel game with us, trying to trick us. However, God does allow us to live in a world where we are constantly tempted and, according to Scripture, there is a purpose. After all, Jesus Himself had to live within a world of temptation.

Hebrews 5:8 says that Jesus, though a Son, learned obedience through what He suffered. At first glance, this verse is a bit hard to understand. Why would Jesus, the perfect and sinless Son of God, need to learn anything? But when the Bible speaks of Jesus learning obedience, it is referring to the experience and application of obedience. It's not as though Jesus was previously disobedient and had to then become obedient. The verse means that with every trial and temptation Jesus faced, He both applied and then experienced obedience in the face of evil alternatives. The point is, it wasn't just a theoretical obedience but an actual obedience demonstrated again and again and again. In this sense He "learned" to obey His Father in the face of daily temptations to do the opposite.

That is why He can sympathize with us, for He knows firsthand what it costs to choose the hard way of truth over the easier path of lies. We are not sinless, but by God's grace, we are forgiven and we learn obedience within a world of temptation.

The presence of temptation is not the problem—it's our failure to recognize it.

But wait, in the Sermon on the Mount, didn't Jesus tell us to pray, "Lead us not into temptation"? Yes, He did. But let us understand the meaning of it. To pray what Jesus tells us is to say, "God, keep me from turning this situation of testing into a sinful one." Though God allows us to live in the midst of temptation, He is not the one responsible for our desire to do evil within it. His purpose is that we would learn to depend on Him in every situation. Satan's design is to appeal to our fallen nature and lure us from God with custom-made temptations, inviting us to stray.

God, on the other hand, appeals to our new nature, our true identity in Christ, inviting us to obey.

Our view of temptation cannot be too narrow, as though God were absent from us in our moment of need, or as though He were unaware that Satan is seeking our downfall. No, He has promised to be with us and to walk us through all the wilderness experiences. Though temptation is authored by Satan for our destruction, it's allowed by God for our training. It plays a role in our progress, maturity, and character—in who we will become.

AN EXERCISE CALLED TEMPTATION

If you ever want to read Christian material that is spicy, dramatic, and packed full of truth, just read sermons from seventeenth-century English preachers. Picture them passionately preaching to women in their funny bonnets and men in their strange black ties, who tremble with awe on those old wooden benches as they listen. John Owen was one of those ministers, and what he had to say about temptation is profound. He said, "Temptation is like a knife, that may either cut the meat or the throat of a man; it may be his food or his poison, his exercise or his destruction."[2]

I'm sure we have all thought of temptation as being our poison or destruction—but have we ever thought of it as being food or exercise?

I believe that this is what we are taught when we read about the testing of Jesus in the wilderness. On the one hand, we must be warned that temptation can lead to destruction. But on the other hand, temptation can catapult us into deeper growth, if we learn to trust God in the midst of it.

If we learn to lean on truth in the face of a lie.

At first glance, the three temptations Jesus faces in the wilderness seem so … unexpected. At least they seemed that way to me for a long time. I mean, I would imagine that if we were going to be given a crash course on temptation with Jesus as our leader, it would take place in some type of ancient Las Vegas, where sex, drugs, and rock and roll abound. Isn't that why some people call it Sin City? But then again, it could also take place in Salt Lake City, with its temples, anti-coffee policies, and religious undergarments. If we really believe what the Bible says about sin, then it could really be anywhere. Even in a wilderness.

We need to understand what it is about the temptation to turn rocks to bread, jump off a Jerusalem tower, and view the glory of world kingdoms that teaches us about the nature of temptation itself and how we are to face it. Understanding temptation's heart-revealing effect enables us to look at the account of Christ's temptation in Matthew 4 with fresh eyes. What does it teach us about the lies of Satan? And about the deepest need of the human heart? And the true identity of Jesus? And how does this connect to the rest of the New Testament teaching about our justification, the power of the Holy Spirit, and what it means for our character? These are crucial questions.

Each temptation contains a lie, which, if believed, weakens our spiritual health and leads us down a destructive path, away from what God intends. Yet each temptation can also be an opportunity to step further into Christ's life-giving victory, launching us deeper into our true identity as the beloved of God.

Yes, within us we have competing commitments and conflicting desires. We want to sacrificially love other people, and yet we are drawn toward self-centeredness. We want to be faithful to our spouses, and yet we are tempted with unfaithful thoughts. We want to follow Christ in daily life, and yet we feel the pull to follow our fallen passions. But the truth of God's grace in Jesus makes it possible to change, to be transformed to become Christlike.

Temptation is an enemy.

Surprisingly, it can become our growth opportunity.

Each time we choose truth in the face of a lie, we are, in a sense, flexing muscles in our spiritual lives that grow stronger with each challenge. The result is that we become more mature, our character grows, and by God's grace, we reflect the beauty of Jesus to those around us. Every moment of temptation can be an exercise in what matters most. These moments don't have to kill you. They can make you stronger.

chapter four

WHEN INDEPENDENCE LIES

And after fasting forty days and forty nights, he was hungry.
And the tempter came and said to him, "If you are the Son of
God, command these stones to become loaves of bread." But
he answered, "It is written, 'Man shall not live by bread alone,
but by every word that comes from the mouth of God.'"

Matthew 4:2–4

Nancy always looked calm and collected, which is what made her confession all the more shocking. After months of giving the impression that everything was fine, she admitted to being plagued with thoughts of self-destruction. She did not want to admit them to anyone. Yet holding them in was becoming toxic for her, destructive from the inside out.

The day she told me was right after a Sunday morning church service. We immediately prayed together, and her tears began to flow and I could sense God working. After saying "Amen" I told her that she had to promise to tell the people she knew in the church right away. At first, she resisted. She didn't want to be seen as a person "in need." She said, "I've always just done this on my own. I don't want to be dependent on others. I have to prove that I'm strong." She had believed a lie that she didn't need to be dependent on anyone.

I simply told her, "All of us are needy. I am needy, and none of us can live the life God has called us to on our own. We just need to admit it and be amazed by the help God gives us by His Spirit and through His people." That afternoon Nancy told three people in the church, who thankfully showed great compassion and care. She said it was the best decision she had made in months.

I generally hate to admit areas of vulnerability. I try to cover them up, play them down, and minimize them in order to give the appearance of having it all together. When asked how I am doing, I respond with the general, "I'm great/well/busy/good."

But vulnerable?

Rarely.

The easiest lie to believe is the lie that says we don't need help—after all, we can do this on our own, we're "captain of our own souls," and all that. This mind-set of independence lies beneath the surface of many of our decisions and so many areas of our lives that we must give it careful thought. Though it can appear to look like freedom, it actually keeps us from it. The truth is that we are all in great need, and though we may at times be unwilling to admit it, we are still vulnerable.

What stops us from confessing it?

Vulnerability is not our enemy; it's our opportunity.

The only areas of weakness that will keep us from growth are the ones we won't admit.

The first lie Jesus faces in the wilderness doesn't actually sound much like a lie at all; it sounds more like a suggestion. Up to this point in the story, Jesus has been alone in the wilderness without food for forty days, to pray out of obedience to and dependence on His Father. Naturally, He is starving.

The Devil sees this area of vulnerability and suggests a solution that doesn't sound so bad on the surface.

After all, how could a little carb indulgence be so wrong?

EXPLOITING OUR WEAKNESS

As legend has it, young Robert Johnson took his guitar to the crossroads of Highways 49 and 61 in Clarksdale, Mississippi, to have it tuned by the Devil. What Johnson wanted was not all that different from what we all probably want at some point in our lives—a little taste of immortality and incredible ability. Johnson wanted to transcend his life of poverty and anonymity into one of power—power over audiences that the guitar would allow him to wield. He was met on the road by a large, dark figure who taught him the guitar in exchange for his soul. Many a Christian has been suspicious of good guitar playing ever since.

But the guitar was just a vehicle for the story. While a lush and beautiful instrument, it can become just another vehicle to prove our worth, to show off our significance, to leave a legacy. In that, it's not all that different from money, sex, possessions, power, and position. It just happened to be what Robert Johnson had on him at the time.

And, the story goes, in order to fully master the instrument and prove his worth, Robert was willing to sell the most important part of himself.

This idea of making a pact with the Devil is a reoccurring theme in religious circles. It reflects what many of us think temptation to be—a dramatic, obvious spiritual transaction in which the Prince of Darkness offers us goods and services at the mere cost of our souls. The truth is that it often looks less dramatic and much more subtle.

Believing lies rarely feels as if you're selling your soul.

It may even feel like you are gaining your freedom.

Why else would we believe them so easily?

If you wanted to deceive someone and influence that person against his or her better judgment, you probably would not say, "Hey, you, do something terrible. Seriously. Curse God and kill a kitten." You would use a different tactic—something much more clever that flies under the radar, which is precisely what happens here.

The problem with Satan's miracle bread solution is that it's contrary to God's plan at that time for Jesus. This is what the Enemy is always presenting, an alternative plan to God's. Here he is seeking to lure the Son of God away from His Father, and the Devil attempts the same for us. So what is his strategy? Exploit weakness, undermine priorities, and appeal to our independence. How are we to guard against this?

The answer isn't becoming defensive; it's being vulnerable.

Naturally, we think that the best way for us to guard our areas of weakness is by acting as though we don't have them. If there were a modern self-help library available in the wilderness that day, I suppose the books would be titled *You've Got This!* or *Never Weak Again!* Notice, however, what Jesus doesn't do. When Satan says,

"Make some bread," Jesus doesn't say, "I'm fine Satan, really. I'm not hungry anyway. I just didn't feel like eating for a month."

Jesus, though fully God, is also fully man, and He is aware of what His body is going through. This, I believe, is something that the church must get right if we are to become who God wants us to be. *Confessing weakness and vulnerability is not a sin.* In fact, acknowledging them can become a strength. Jesus did not pretend that His body didn't need food. In the wilderness He is demonstrating His vulnerability to human weakness and suffering. Acknowledging areas of vulnerability is key in overcoming lies.

Developing a culture of vulnerability is essential to the Christian life. Though I was initially caught off guard, I came to love the raw and real approach to the Christian life I learned while I was on staff at the church that would eventually send me out to plant a new church in Los Angeles in 2005. The leadership was very deliberate about creating a culture of transparency and openness, and it had a transformative effect for my wife and me. Daily, I was asked about the health of my marriage, if I needed help in parenting, or if I needed some personal encouragement. It's an incredible source of strength and encouragement to me when I am around other people who are aware of my strengths and weaknesses and who seek to help me. I become a little less prone to listen to the whispered lies of Satan when other strong voices are speaking truth into my life.

Sadly, this isn't the experience for many Christians, but shouldn't it be? I don't think this kind of openness and honesty should be seen as an optional extra for "heavy users" of Christianity; vulnerable community should be the norm. This does not mean that you are constantly with others, who are by your side for twenty-four hours a day. But fostering vulnerable community when you are with others becomes powerfully strengthening for the times when you are alone.

Some of the greatest tests in life take place when no one else is watching. Dwight L. Moody once said, "Character is what you are in the dark." Being alone can be both a blessing and a battlefield. That day in the wild, Jesus was not enjoying a feast with His followers. Neither was He surrounded by a crowd of listeners; He was alone. Satan knew this. In fact, part of his strategy was that he waited to tempt Jesus in His solitude and in His need. Why? Because Satan not only seeks to exploit our *condition*, but he also takes advantage of our *situation*.

We must be open before others, and ultimately, we must be open before God. Are we prone to anxiety? Depression? Lust? Greed? And are these areas more tempting when we are alone? Opening yourself up to God and others about areas of weakness is not a loss; it becomes a win. Admitting an area of weakness can cause you to trust in the strength that God Himself supplies. Isn't that what the apostle Paul said? When I am weak, then I am strong because I'm not depending upon myself any longer, but upon God Himself (2 Cor. 12:9–10)! The whispered suggestions of the Enemy are intended to exploit weakness in order to do what he really wants to do, to act independently of God.

UNDERMINING OUR PRIORITIES

I've noticed something interesting about temptation within the city where I pastor. Los Angeles is a place that draws all kinds of people from across the United States, and even the world. Some who have grown up in a conservative environment, perhaps even grown up in a church, simply adopt a moral code of behavior that has been passed down to them by their parents or culture. But it's not actually rooted in *conviction*; it's merely an *assumption*. They have never really looked into these for themselves. When temptation comes, it all gets revealed.

Imagine you've just moved to Hollywood and (just to use a stereotype) someone says, "Hey! Welcome to LA! Let's do drugs!" You respond by saying, "Well, I would but God says I can't." Sounds more like frustration than conviction. See, if I just adopt a moral code but I don't know its source or its significance, then it's just an assumption. I will get tangled up in confusion and second-guessing when temptation comes.

If you are not convinced that the job of a sea captain is to secure the safety of his or her crew and passengers, then you might end up being the first to leave when the ship is sinking. Priorities are decisions settled in your heart before opportunities. If you are not convinced of the reason you stand, you will surely fall when the alternative comes. It's when "I can't" changes to "I won't" that we have moved from assumption to conviction.

By fasting, Jesus was being obedient to God. Satan wants to weaken this commitment. This is really the heart of the matter. The temptation begins with questions of weakness: "Why are you hungry?," then slowly moves toward questions of priorities, "Why are you fasting in the first place?"

This is where we must be clear about Satan's goal in temptation. It's not merely to get us to do something bad. His goal is to turn us away from our true identity as God's people. That is precisely what he is doing when he says, "If you are the Son of God …," hinting that there is some doubt about whether or not Jesus really is in fact the Son of God. What better way, then, Satan suggests, than for Jesus to show off His own strength? Satan's offer has the appearance of strength and independence, but it's simply a temptation to prove oneself … by oneself. It's the temptation to be sub-Christian. It undermines the greatest priority in the universe: God.

Imagine someone who works in a high position of government is presented with an opportunity to turn a blind eye in order to make some extra cash. It's an opportunity to make money at the expense of the people in that city or state. In that moment the temptation is to elevate lesser things (his or her own wallet) at the expense of greater things (justice for the people).

Every day we are faced with alternatives that undermine priorities.

The Enemy will always elevate lesser things to ultimate status. Jesus had a purpose for why He was there and what He was doing; it was a call and commitment to fasting in the wilderness. Satan undermines this by saying, "Isn't making bread for Yourself more important than obeying God?" If the Enemy can call into question what is most important, then he can convince us to look elsewhere to get what we truly need. Even if, *especially* if, it means looking away from God.

But subtlety is key. The whispered suggestions of the Enemy will rarely tell us to look away from God; he is much more effective when he simply suggests we look to ourselves.

APPEALING TO INDEPENDENCE

Divorce is never pretty, but it's especially ugly when the two parties are spewing venom at each other and everyone else. As a pastor, I am often a witness to situations like this, in which the husband and wife are so adamantly against each other that it's as if you are watching a verbal boxing match. How does it get to this point? How does, for example, the man I knew from our church get to the point where he leaves not only his wife but also his little daughter? I would suggest that it begins with entitlement. This particular man was becoming very successful in the legal world of the entertainment industry. It seemed as though every pleasure under the sun was being thrown at him and the red carpet was rolled out for him. He slowly began to believe it was okay for him to indulge in whatever he desired and that he deserved it. This explains the outrage his wife faced when she finally confronted him on his sins. He was so upset, so appalled that anyone would call into question his right to do whatever he wanted. Everyone else had to face the wrath.

"*Why shouldn't I?* After all, I *deserve* it!" is usually how the inner dialogue goes in a moment of temptation. I know it well; I hear it every time I pass by my favorite shops. But of course, it's much broader than that—it's the conversations we have within ourselves that shape which direction we will go. And one of the strongest factors in tipping us toward independence from God is entitlement.

When Satan suggested Jesus turn stones into bread to prove He was the Messiah, it's as if Satan were saying, "Why wouldn't You? I mean, after all, You are the Messiah … right? It's within Your power to do so. This whole fasting thing … it's really beneath You, to suffer like that."

Sound familiar? I hear this voice all the time. Sometimes it wins.

Entitlement is a powerful force in our culture, a cocktail mix of part need, part want, and a lot of pride. Many are under its influence. I think we would all agree that the divorce scenario I mentioned is so obviously wrong, and we might even assume that we would never do something like that. Yet we tend to overlook the driving force behind it, which is the entitlement that brings someone to that place. Remember, Jesus wasn't being tempted with sex, drugs, and rock and roll; He was just tempted with bread. The point, however, was to get the Son of God to act independently of His Father, to satisfy His own needs at the expense of trusting His Father. It's similar for us—Satan wants us to believe that God is optional, that we are "above" Him. For if you don't ultimately depend on God, then you are depending on something else. You now have an idol. It's a temptation to build a life on anything less than God, to live in a way that God never intended, to live in the subspiritual.

How do we understand Jesus's response to this temptation? A little Old Testament context here is helpful. In this wilderness scene, Jesus is about to quote a passage from the book of Deuteronomy, chapter 8, a word that was given to the nation of Israel reminding them of who God is, what He's done for them, what He shall do for them, and how they're not to turn away from Him. They must not forget God; they're to remember that He is *Creator*, that they are *creation*. And there's a warning to the people of Israel that essentially says, "Be careful lest your heart become proud and you look around at all that you have and you say, 'By my own hand I have brought this for myself.'" Make no mistake, bread is not bad. Jesus told us to pray for our daily bread. In fact, later on in Jesus's ministry, He miraculously provides bread for thousands in need! What makes Satan's proposal, well, satanic, is the idea that bread could be separated from the One who provides it.

GOD'S WORD DEFINES LIFE

We are dependent creatures. We need food, water, shelter, and relationships. We need God. The great lie believed in secular society is that we are independent of God, looking to enjoy the gift of life without acknowledging a Giver. Every day we are being told by marketing campaigns, books, podcasts, and so on that the missing ingredient for unleashing unlimited liberation is found from within. It may sound like freedom, but in fact, it's self-destruction. Here at the outset we discover Satan's goal in temptation: it's to turn us away from our true identity and purpose, not just to get us to do something bad. Jesus unmasks this lie and teaches us what true freedom is.

In the midst of temptation, Jesus elevates the conversation above the subspiritual by appealing to what is far, far greater than meeting a momentary need. He appeals to the written Word of God. He answers, "It is written, 'Man shall not live by bread alone, but by every word that comes from the mouth of God'" (Matt. 4:4).

Here is our secret resource in the midst of temptation (though it's not actually secret at all; we just easily forget). Holy Scripture is called "the sword of the Spirit" (Eph. 6:17) by the apostle Paul, an offensive weapon of truth against the lies of sin. Notice how Jesus wields it. He is directing Scripture not only at the Enemy but also toward Himself, showing us that in moments of temptation, we must remember this truth: we are defined by what our Creator has declared, not merely by what we desire.

Scripture gives us our worldview. For Jesus, it defines life. We must learn to utilize Scripture in such a way that recognizes its authority. God has revealed Himself and His purposes for humanity through holy Scripture. He connects us to a larger story, a greater meaning, a bigger purpose than ourselves and our individual appetites. Meet your temptations with the truth. Each time you choose to step into the direction of God in a moment of temptation, you actually become more of who God wants you to be.

GOD'S WORD IS DIVINE NOURISHMENT

The book of Proverbs speaks about how words have the power to bring life or death; they can be like a bitter poison or a satisfying meal. Just think of the last argument you were in or the last encouragement you received, and you will be reminded of this very quickly. Have you ever had words spoken to you that, when you listened to them, you felt as if you had eaten a fantastic meal? Words from family or friends so uplifting, so encouraging, so helpful, so loving and kind that when you heard them, you just felt whole and *full*?

We get a taste of this when a friend says, "You are such a gift to me!" or your child says, "I love you!" If the words of others can feel like a satisfying meal, then how much more should we feed off the written Word of God? Jesus's point is this: just as one dies physically without physical nourishment, one will also die spiritually and eternally without spiritual nourishment.

Without it, we're lost.

Just imagine your heart and mind as a giant food pantry that is empty, waiting to be filled. God comes along and says, "Here! Here is My Word! Take, eat, feast!" How do we feast? By chewing on the incredible truths written for us. Truths that tell us we have been made in the image of God and we become new creations in Christ; truths declaring how God's love and favor have been lavished upon us as free gifts. These are the meals of grace. They are not empty words or vague ideas; they are proven truth that communicates God's love.

We are now being elevated beyond the subspiritual. The satisfaction of physical hunger that only bread can comfort cannot begin to compare to the satisfaction of how God meets our spiritual hunger: "Man shall not live by bread alone, but by every word that comes from the mouth of God." There is a giant, spiritual famine in our world. We need nourishment. Every word that comes pouring out of the mouth of God is to be the greatest nourishment of our lives.

When you truly love someone, you gladly surrender. When a person falls in love, for example, he or she might use words such as, "I will do anything for [insert name]!" or "There's no one else I'd rather be with!" As human beings, we are designed to give ourselves gladly to the people we love. We feed on thoughts of them throughout our day, and this shapes the choices we make. Something was filling Jesus's mind and flooding His heart when He was hungry in the wilderness. When fasting from food, He was feasting on His Father's love. We are invited to this feast.

GOD'S PROVEN LOVE

Sometimes chapter and verse numbers in our printed Bibles can disconnect us from the whole context. I want to make a connection that precedes the beginning of Matthew 4. With the wilderness temptation clearly in our minds, I now want you to consider what took place at the end of chapter 3, beginning in verse 16, when Jesus was baptized publicly. It says, "And when Jesus was baptized, immediately he went up from the water, and behold, the heavens were opened to him, and he saw the Spirit of God descending like a dove and coming to rest on him; and behold, a voice from heaven said, 'This is my beloved Son, with whom I am well pleased.'" It was then, and from there, that Jesus was led by the Spirit into the wilderness to be tempted by the Devil.

Before He faced the voice of Satan, He heard the voice of His Father.

The word that His Father had spoken over Him was His food. He was so confident in the love of the Father for Him that He went forward into moments of testing and temptation, and proved His love for the Father in glad surrender. When you love something, you gladly surrender to it, and Jesus did this in glad surrender, thus proving His love for the Father, because He knew the Father's love for Him. If it's true that the decisions you make in moments of temptation demonstrate what you truly value, then what does that demonstrate about Jesus? He loves His Father.

The temptation was aimed, as it is for us, at splitting the relationship. What is the glue that keeps it together? Love. The glue is love. The Father loved Him, He loved the Father, and in Christ we are loved! The same words that the Father spoke over Jesus are spoken over all those who believe in Him: "This is my beloved child, in whom I am well pleased."

It's the only approval we need.

And it was from this position that Jesus went in, filled by the Spirit, to face temptation. And we are to go out in the same way—filled with the confidence of God's love for us.

This is a missing ingredient in the conversation about temptation. Oftentimes we focus only on the "no" in temptation, the thing we shouldn't do. We must also look at the "yes." Look at how good God is and how wonderful God is, and how loving and kind and righteous and just! Whenever God calls you to say no, it's always for a greater yes.

And what was the "yes" that Jesus was saying here? "Yes, Father, I am going to perform the mission You have called Me to in sacrificial service." Up to this point in Matthew's gospel, Jesus has been declared as the Messiah, but what kind of Messiah would He be? Would He be a selfish Messiah? Or would He come in sacrificial service? Jesus, in resisting the shortcut offered to Him by Satan, says, "Yes, I will lay My life down."

If decisions in moments of temptation demonstrate what we truly value, and Jesus was willing to deny Himself, not just in the wilderness but all the way to the point of a cross, what does that say about you? It says you are loved. It's because of Christ's work that you and I can hear the same voice, the voice of the Father speaking over us: "This is my beloved child, in whom I am well pleased."

If you have heard the truth from heaven, you can face all the lies of hell.

PERFECT LOVE FOR IMPERFECT CIRCUMSTANCES

In the beginning, in the garden of Eden, Adam and Eve severed their special relationship by giving in to temptation. And they did it in the most ideal circumstances. How many of us have thought we wouldn't give in so readily if we just had better circumstances?

Adam and Eve had everything. They were living the dream, naked and unashamed together, in the presence of God. Everything was epic, organic, fair trade, free range, and positively delicious. And yet in the most ideal circumstances, they failed and fell into temptation.

It's not about finding the perfect circumstance; it doesn't exist. It's about having the perfect Savior.

Jesus, in the worst of circumstances, out in the wilderness, alone, without food, with the beasts—and Satan—conquers. He overcomes. Jesus stood where Adam and Eve fell; Jesus stood where Israel fell; Jesus stood where Moses fell; and Jesus stood where you fall. All so that you could be lifted up. So that you could be renewed. So that you could walk in victory.

If we have caved in to the power of luring lies, there is forgiveness in Christ and there's power in the Spirit. Patterning your life choices on these truths is absolutely essential. Our resistance to sin and temptation must be rooted in our love for God. And our love for God is rooted in His love for us shown in Jesus. That is why Jesus said, "I am the bread of life." Knowing ourselves to be dependent people leads to delivered lives.

The pressure to act independently of God often stems from our desire to prove ourselves, to prove our worth. There are so many voices around us saying, "Prove yourself! Prove yourself!" This was the voice of Satan to Christ: "Prove Yourself to be God's beloved: turn these stones to bread." To this, as writer Henri Nouwen reminds us, Jesus says, "No, I don't have to prove anything. I am already the Beloved."[1]

When you and I look to the cross, we, too, can say, "I don't have to prove myself. I am the beloved of God."

chapter five

A HABITAT FOR DIVINITY

If the Spirit of him who raised Jesus from the dead dwells in
you, he who raised Christ Jesus from the dead will also give life
to your mortal bodies through his Spirit who dwells in you.

Romans 8:11

Among the many ways you could choose to torment an elementary
schoolboy of eight, one of the most effective by far is the Suzuki
method. Developed more than a hundred years ago by a Japanese
violinist as a way of teaching music to children, it's been praised by
countless teachers and students, decade after decade. For me, however, it was death. I was told it was as easy as "following the lesson,"
but I just wasn't learning. My recollections of pounding the ivories in
that cold, sterile practice room were not positive. I remember wish-
ing that somehow Shin'ichi Suzuki himself would resurrect and help
me in person. He didn't, of course, and in the end, I gave up piano
in favor of guitar.

At least I could look cooler while practicing to Guns N' Roses
in the mirror.

Take that, Suzuki.

As Christians, we often feel as I did learning the piano. You hear "Follow the example of Jesus" and you instantly feel frustrated—even exhausted. As we think about Jesus victoriously overcoming the lies of Satan in the wilderness, we learn a lot about the nature of temptation. But how on earth can we face it ourselves? I'll be honest. I begin to lose heart even thinking about fasting for more than a couple of days, let alone forty! But this is precisely how the gospel gives us hope.

Unlike Suzuki—who could never have sent me supernatural power to play Beethoven—Jesus, and faith in Him, provides the power we need to face the daily temptations of life. Christ hasn't just left us with a lesson; He has left us with a Helper. His name is the Holy Spirit.

When I was a brand-new Christian, I thought that only certain believers had the power to resist temptation. In my mind there were two classes of Christians—normal (me and my friends) and *next-level* (everybody else). Normal Christians couldn't really overcome anything; they fell into temptation all the time and were otherwise destined to live a mediocre Christian life. Then, I thought, there were the next-level Christians. These were like supercharged, extra holy, privileged Christians who had power to overcome.

Thank God I was dead wrong. I read through the book of Romans for the first time, overwhelmed by the promise that through faith God inhabits every believer and gives you the power you need to live like Jesus. The Holy Spirit's power is not the privilege of special believers but the promise to every believer.

In the first century, early Christians heard the same message. They weren't told to "follow the example of Jesus" in their own strength.

They were told of God's promised Spirit who would dwell in them and empower them. This is what the early church in Rome heard when Paul wrote his letter. After explaining the truth and power of Christ's work accomplished for fallen humanity, Paul begins to tell of the resources available to every Christian.

Before we continue to look at Christ in His wilderness temptation, we must know all that we need to face our temptation, conquer sin, and walk in holiness brought to us by the Spirit.

He doesn't just show up now and then, so we don't need to fear His absence.

In fact, He makes you His new home.

YOU ARE GOD'S RESIDENCE

Every parent has guilty pleasures. These are the things parents love to do when the kids are finally asleep or when they are gone on a weekend getaway. They are typically the dullest and most unremarkable things you could think of.

For my wife and me, it's binge watching HGTV.

I hate to admit it, but there is something so appealing about watching previously uninhabitable homes become residences that reflect the character of their new owners.

This is what happens when God dwells in us. Writer Melanie Rainer comments on the popularity of renovation shows, saying, "We love renovation stories because they echo the desire in all of us to be rediscovered and remade. We're all a work in a progress, each of us a fixer-upper in our own right. We see ourselves in tired old homes and long for a life-saving gospel renovation in our own hearts."[1] Because of the power of the gospel, we who are uninhabitable because of sin become a dwelling place for God, a habitat for divinity.

When my oldest daughter was five, she would ask the best/cutest questions about God and the Bible. One day, as we were reading a lesson on how Jesus comes into your life, she asked, "Daddy, how does Jesus get into your heart? I mean, does He just walk in?"

It's actually a very important theological point. How does Jesus dwell in us? Jesus is not in our hearts physically; He dwells in our hearts *by the Spirit*. That is what Jesus was talking about when He shared His final meal before the cross with His followers. He said, "It is to your advantage that I go away" (John 16:7).

What? Why? The disciples in that moment were no doubt perplexed. How could anything be better than the physical, bodily presence of Jesus? Well, it was to their advantage that Jesus enter heaven because then, and only then, once He had accomplished all that was necessary for our salvation through the cross, could He be with them 24-7. This is possible through the third Person of the trinity, who, in Paul's letter to Romans, is referred to as the "Spirit of God," the "Spirit of him who raised Jesus from the dead," and also the "Spirit of Christ."

One of the highlights of these cheesy house-renovation shows (in case you are on the edge of your seat to find out) is the remodeling process. Once the owners get the keys, they draw up plans, hire workers, and begin to transform their new house into a home. One of Paul's important points in the famous eighth chapter of Romans is just that: Once God has taken up residence in a believer, He doesn't stop there. He begins a process. This is what we need to face temptation with hope. A deeper awareness of God's presence in us will always lead to a great demonstration of God's power through us. Like a newly purchased home that begins to take on the character of its owner, we begin to take on the character of our God. He is turning His new house into a home.

THE RENOVATION HAS BEGUN

If you have ever lived in a house or apartment while it's being worked on, then you have a small picture of what Christian growth can be like. Sometimes it's messy. Sometimes it's painful. But it's always for a purpose.

The Latin term from which *renovate* is derived means "making new." God isn't at work making us a little better or a little different; He is in the process of making us new. But we all know that old habits die hard and old patterns can be difficult to break, which is why this renovating process can feel a little painful at times. But we have to admit that sometimes we are the ones that make it difficult. A lot of that has to do with our expectations.

A friend emailed a story a while back about how Pope John Paul II died, went to heaven, and reported back to earth with disappointment. It's not real, of course, but it was hilarious.[2] The story goes that when the pope dies, he gets to heaven and is let down by the lack of stained-glass windows, marble statues, and gold ceilings. "If I'd known heaven would be like this," he says, "I would've taken one last tour through my 50 rooms of velvet-draped thrones." The idea, which is quite funny, is that the pope's standards exceeded heaven's.

The reality, oddly enough, is that the reverse is actually true. Many of our frustrations with God's renovating process don't come from expectations that are too high, but too low! Now, I am not saying that you should expect God to drop gold mansions from heaven on your property; rather, I am talking about the character of your life. We settle for just little tweaks and additions here and there, when God's plan is not a touch-up but a gut renovation. A house being redesigned by God will look more and more like Jesus.

My wife and I used to own a home in the East Hollywood area of LA. It was old, built around 1921, and it was on the side of a small hill. One day I noticed cracks appearing on the walls and the back door started to stick. At first I tried to just cover up the cracks and adjust the door, but it kept getting worse. It wasn't until I went under the house that I realized the whole foundation wall at the back of the house was cracked. It took too many weeks and way too much money to fix it.

Like my cracked foundation wall, some of our biggest problems are the ones we are not aware of. The cracks in the wall did not create the problem—they revealed the problem. The constant temptation in the Christian life is to deal only with surface issues, as though the problem were just a little crack in the wall. Perhaps this is why so many Christians are not desperate for or dependent on God's power—they don't see the need for it! Satan would love nothing more than a bunch of unempowered Christians. The way he tries to accomplish this is by convincing us that the problem of sin isn't really that bad, that we can take care of it on our own. All the while, there is a deeper issue beneath the surface.

This is when temptation can become an opportunity. When we start to see little cracks in our behavior or our attitudes, we shouldn't overlook them as though they don't matter. Instead, we should take an honest look at what Scripture has to say about the flaws; for underneath them are desires and drives that God wants to transform. The answer is not to pretend that so-called "small sins" don't really matter. There are only small sins if there is a small God. They need to be seen for what they are.

Temptation has a way of revealing issues that you thought were nonexistent. Though Satan's goal, as we have learned, is to exploit our weaknesses in order to defeat us, God allows this process in order to heal us. Through repentance we destroy the works of Satan. In the next chapter we will think practically about what that looks like and how that happens. But know this: those little cracks are reminders to us of how much we need our God.

These moments of temptation can reveal spiritual reality. When we are drawn toward things that are anti-God, we need to look beneath the surface and ask the "why" question. *Why is that appealing to me? What do I hope to gain from disobeying God?* For example, when I feel unrighteous anger welling up inside of me, the Holy Spirit enters that inner dialogue taking place in my heart. *Why am I giving in to this kind of anger right now?* God reveals to me that I am angry because I feel unappreciated, undervalued, and not in control. As the Spirit brings the truth of Scripture to bear on my heart, however, I am reminded that I should not give in to this anger, that I am accepted by God in grace and don't have to be in control of this particular situation because I know He is. It would be very easy for us in these situations to just pass it off as no big deal. But it's a big deal.

If I don't recognize this truth and submit to it, I start going down a dark path. No wonder Paul wrote to the Ephesians, "Do not let the sun go down on your anger, and give no opportunity to the devil" (4:26–27).

These times are pivotal for our growth. The Holy Spirit enters the inner dialogue of our hearts and reminds us that we belong to God, that there is nothing that we truly need that He does not provide. While we are looking to deal with little cosmetic touch-ups, God is rebuilding the foundation. The more you become aware of how great and deep the problem of sin is, the more you rejoice in the One who can fix it. And He cares about every detail because He is making you a home for Himself.

THE POWER IS THE RELATIONSHIP

Before I was married, I was obsessed with musical recording equipment. You see, there was this period of time called the nineties, and those who lived in this decade were restricted to primitive recording devices that required such things as wires and cables. My room was so full of them that you couldn't even see the floor. It looked like the lab of a mad scientist. I was totally comfortable with it. But I knew the day I got married that my wife would NOT be okay with my mess/genius. It had to go.

I'm still trying to get over it.

Living with someone, whether a spouse or a roommate, or living with family brings both intimacy and difficulty. I remember the early days when my wife and I first got married—how we discovered all sorts of things about each other that the previous two years of dating did not reveal. You see what he or she sees and experience what he or she experiences when you are in the same dwelling place. All my habits that were previously acceptable to me (such as leaving the toothpaste cap off or leaving some dirty clothes on the floor) were no longer acceptable because of the presence of another.

When we think about God's renovation process, we must keep this in mind: it's relationship. God is not flipping you so He can put you back on the market. He has come to renovate you that He might be with you.

Relationship is the goal, both now and in eternity. And we do not want to grieve Him. God must expel the things that are contrary to His nature, the things that grieve Him. His presence in us and His relationship with us reveal many areas of life that are in need of renewal. It is for the sake of greater and deeper intimacy that God is getting rid of sin and snares in your life.

This is precisely the point where the Devil attacks. Temptations will be designed, as they were with Jesus in the wilderness, to split the relationship between you and God. Satan may very well understand that he can't own you—you have been purchased by the blood of Jesus Christ. But if he can't terminate the ownership, he will seek to disrupt the intimacy. These attacks often come in the most subtle forms, seeking to distract you and deter you from living out of intimacy with your Father in heaven.

Not long after my conversion, I moved away from the San Francisco Bay Area to attend a Bible college in Southern California. One of the first books I was given to read by one of my roommates was a classic book on spiritual warfare by Warren Wiersbe called *The Strategy of Satan*. I will never forget reading it because the introduction was instantly engaging. At the beginning of the book, there is a word of warning: "No doubt Satan will do everything he can to keep you from benefiting from this book. He will distract you and detour you. He will seek to confuse you, or perhaps make you critical. He will arrange interruptions. I suggest you ask the Lord for his help and protection as you study these pages."[3]

I have found those words to be absolutely true ever since. We would all do well to heed them. Just as Jesus depended on His special relationship with His Father in every temptation, we now, through Jesus, have an intimate relationship with our Father. And just as the tempter sought to sever the relationship between Father and Son, he will seek to do it with us. The greatest defense against temptation is intimacy with God.

The book of Revelation contains a well-known but often misunderstood letter from Jesus to a lukewarm church. He says to the church of Laodicea that they boast and brag about the relationship they have, when in fact they are not engaged in it. So in the middle of this particular letter, He says these words to the church—and perhaps to us—"Behold, I stand at the door and knock. If anyone hears my voice and opens the door, I will come in to him and eat with him, and he with me" (3:20).

Some Christians think that this is an evangelistic text, but He is actually speaking to the *church*. To those He loves, He corrects and rebukes. He is not saying that the church has become un-Christian or unsaved; He is saying that the church is His house, but He is not being let in. There is ownership but no intimacy. They claimed to have it when in fact they had lost it. Revelation 3:20 is not an invitation to conversion; it's an invitation to communion.

ENJOY WHAT IS YOURS

Let's face it, one of the great temptations we fall into is hypocrisy. We believe the lie that as long as we put on masks in front of other Christians, everything will be okay. When in fact, on the inside we might feel bitterness, anger, and disappointment toward God. We are not actually enjoying the very thing we claim to have.

God has not just left us with a lesson; He has given us a relationship. What is best for you and everyone around you is intimacy with Him. In fact, one of the reasons you may be experiencing so many difficulties in the relationships around you is because you are not allowing Christ to truly "dwell" in your heart. I once heard a leader say that although the Holy Spirit may be present in every believer, He is not always preeminent. If we aren't aware of this, we will begin to blame all other kinds of things, people, and circumstances, when in fact it's an intimacy problem.

Jesus gives us a strong but beautiful word: *repent*. Repentance is always good news, for it means turning back to what truly matters. Repentance is not a way of earning something that doesn't belong to you; it's a way of enjoying what already does belong to you.

Imagine a married couple who has not been intimate for some time. There has to be discord and distance. The one spouse says to the other, "Repent, let us become close again." What that spouse is saying is this: "Let us enjoy what is already ours." And that means making room and getting rid of the things that grieve the intimacy, such as "sexual immorality, impurity, passion, evil desire, and covetousness" (Col. 3:5). His love poured out into our hearts by the Spirit is the very reason these things need to go.

The point of all this is for the Spirit to dwell in you. He is re-making you. You are not condemned to learn on your own or lean on your own strength (like me trying to learn piano). He is with you and He empowers you. The same Spirit who raised Jesus from the dead dwells in you! This is what you need to overcome temptation. There will come a day when this new construction is complete and there is no more wreckage and no more decay. This process is now pointing toward an incredible future. You are on your way to glory. Don't let Satan tell you otherwise.

chapter six

WHEN RELIGION LIES

Then the devil took him to the holy city and set him on the pinnacle
of the temple and said to him, "If you are the Son of God, throw
yourself down, for it is written, 'He will command his angels
concerning you,' and 'On their hands they will bear you up, lest
you strike your foot against a stone.'" Jesus said to him, "Again
it is written, 'You shall not put the Lord your God to the test.'"

Matthew 4:5–7

The twenty-six-mile-long Boston Marathon is a well-known en-
durance course, and on April 21, 1980, race history was made. A
twenty-six-year-old New Yorker crossed the finish line with a record-
breaking time of two hours and thirty-one minutes. There was only
one problem. She didn't actually run the race. As she accepted the
winner's wreath on the podium, people quickly began to notice
her lack of perspiration, and race checkpoint officials struggled to
recognize her face. The truth is, she actually jumped in on the final
half mile, decked out in all the official race apparel. But she never
admitted to cheating. Though personally pressed with accusations of
cheating, she insisted that she did not, really believing that she had

legitimately run and won, and stated she would do another marathon for proof.

She never did.

This story is often told to make a point about religiosity; it's like running a race we haven't really entered. We can be wearing the right uniform and appear to be nearing the finish line of a "good life" and yet not actually be in the race at all. The appearance is there, but not the substance. Although we may not live in denial about something as obvious as a marathon, it's nonetheless very easy for us to wear the outfit of religion and be deceived into hypocrisy. It's one of the most common accusations against Christianity, and as a result some people are forever suspicious of any religious institution. The late atheist Christopher Hitchens certainly wasn't hiding his feelings when he said, "Religion poisons everything,"[1] and many would agree. Some of our deepest wounds may have come to us in the name of religion.

And yet, hasn't religion advocated for orphanages, hospitals, and education, and so on? Yes, and that is why author and *New York Times* columnist Ross Douthat says, "America's problem isn't too much religion, or too little of it. It's *bad* religion."[2] For the church, you can trace much of her hypocrisy throughout history to twisted use of Scripture and self-justifying cherry-picking in support of personal agendas. No wonder the seventeenth-century French philosopher Pascal said that men never do evil so completely and cheerfully as when they do it with religious conviction. But here is the thing—it's easy to dismiss this particular temptation as belonging only to medieval crusaders and crooked televangelists, but aren't we also prey?

I personally don't think that anyone just wakes up one morning with a plan to fall into religious temptation. In fact, if and when we do, it might even be somewhat well meaning. A desire for a friend to really follow God can subtly be driven by a desire to control the relationship. A passion for people to receive our prayers can slowly become motivated by a need to be needed. A pursuit of position in the church, though beneficial to others, can secretly be prompted by a deep need to achieve. It's very easy to convince ourselves that we are in the race when all the uniforms look the same. But are we? What is it that our hearts must know about religious temptation so that we are not deceived?

Satan, we have seen, is out to deter Jesus from His true identity and His true mission. And Satan's agenda is the same for us. Though these wilderness temptations are unique to Jesus, they are nonetheless real, and from these accounts we can learn a lot about Satan's strategies and how we can overcome them. If the first temptation was to be sub-Christian, here is a temptation to be super-Christian. If the Devil cannot succeed in making us secular people, he will tempt us as religious people. Unlike the first one, this temptation requires a very specific location and is not nearly as effective without it. Let's call it the "framework" of religious temptation.

HOLY ENVIRONMENT

We are well aware that churches and other religious organizations are capable of deceit and manipulation; after all, people make films about it and TV specials exposing it. And yet, it seems unthinkable that it would happen in our church community, and in our worship services. How could it go wrong? After all, there might be Bibles in the room, scriptures on the walls, Christian bracelets on people's wrists, and worship songs being sung. How could any evil be present in a religious gathering? It seems so unlikely until we remember that Jesus cast out demons not only on the outskirts of cities but also in the synagogues. Apparently, Satan goes to church too.

It's the last place you would ever expect a first-century leader to be tempted. And that is what makes it so diabolical. Satan brings Jesus to the holy city, the city of Jerusalem. He takes Him to the highest point of the temple, right smack in the middle of daily religious life in Israel. A holy temple among holy people.

At first glance, this might seem super random. Doesn't Satan want to keep people away from church? Away from places of worship? Add to that the fact that Satan takes Jesus up as high as possible and then says, "Jump!" What is going on here, and what does it have to do with us? This part of the story used to always confuse me until I realized, what better way for Jesus to launch His public ministry than with a spectacular show of power?

If the first temptation capitalized on what we don't have, this kind of temptation utilizes what we do have. In the first case, there was no food and Jesus was hungry. But in this second temptation, resources surround us: a sacred temple, religious people, holy Scripture. It's familiar, and it's something you probably already know a lot about. Why would Satan try his chances here? Because if he cannot get us in our weakest points, he will then go for our strongest ones. Why is that? Because our strengths are never an obvious target. It's where we least expect temptation to occur. The point is that we rarely suspect a holy environment to become the place of our downfall.

We quickly assume that as long as we are in church—volunteering, leading, perhaps even doing the miraculous—that everything is just fine. Right?

You have probably heard the "sex, drugs, and rock-and-roll" story one thousand times. Man or woman had a freaky past, now comes to church and sings in the choir. But that doesn't necessarily mean there has been a transformation. For some people, it wasn't about the sex and drugs; it was about their influence and status. And when that door of influence closed, they found an open door at a religious institution. It just requires a different outfit. He or she says, "Hey, this is great! I can just come in here, gain position, and people will look to me, need me. And that's wonderful because that's what my life is all about—being needed." Jesus warned on many occasions that there would be people who come into religious environments and gain religious positions, and they would turn out to be wolves in sheep's clothing.

It's very easy to assume that any "higher" or "bigger" or "greater" opportunity or position is always a good thing, especially within the church. We might even talk about them in terms of "blessings." Sometimes they are. But what if that isn't always true? We rarely imagine any situation in which we would use these opportunities or positions for hidden agendas, but we must be careful. Oswald Chambers once said, "An unguarded strength is a double weakness." We must be open and honest not only about our areas of growth but also about our strengths. Of course I'm certainly not saying that all high positions are intrinsically evil. But we underestimate our ability to be driven by ulterior motives and sinful desires. If possible, Satan will try to get you to climb up the religious ladder to a high position with the religious uniform on, and what better place to be than at the top of a holy institution? If Satan cannot get you to fall in secular society, he will get you to rise in religiosity.

MISUSING SCRIPTURE

Imagine a modern-day public relations team trying to represent Jesus in the first century. "First, build Your platform," they would advise, "then do something crazy, something that will make You YouTube famous, like jumping off the highest point of the temple and having angels catch You miraculously! People will love it!" Satan is tempting Jesus to launch His ministry in a spectacular way, and of course, Satan even has Bible verses to support it. In the last temptation, Jesus quoted Scripture against the lies of entitlement and independence. Now, Satan is saying, "Well, I can go to church too! In fact, I think I might try Your church … What's it called? Holy Temple of Jerusalem Church? Oh, I've heard all about it." It's in that very environment that the testing begins. "Jesus," the Devil says, "You trust God? You trust Scripture too, right? How about trusting in Psalm 91?" Satan is now using the Bible. Or I should say, twisting the Bible. Psalm 91 is a psalm about protection. If God will always protect us, then why not throw ourselves into danger? Why don't we force His hand and make Him prove His promises?

I suppose you can make the Bible say anything you want. Just take everything out of context, read your own meaning into it, and you are on your way to starting your very own religion. Twisting Scripture is a classic attribute of religious temptation. I think it was Tennyson who once said a lie that is half truth is the darkest of all lies. That is exactly what Satan is doing in Matthew 4. And there are two ways of doing it.

First up is the *wrong approach*. Before the civil rights movement of the sixties, it was common among some churches to pull out scriptures they thought supported segregation, the dividing up of blacks and whites. "Genesis says," a Bible teacher would say, "that God wants everything to be with its own kind," twisting the meaning of Genesis to support a racist agenda when it's talking about plants, and forgetting that we are all a part of human*kind*. If you want to go down this path, then just ignore the larger narrative, pick what you like, and leave the rest. The problem is that you are left with a paper-doll version of the Bible that you made in your own image.

The second way to twist Scripture is with *wrong application*. Psalm 91, the very thing Satan is quoting to Jesus, is, in fact, about God's care and provision. But here it's being applied in the wrong way. While the people of God can come to expect God's care, we are never to require it in the way we think it should come. Again, Scripture is being used as a tool to support someone's agenda. That, then, gives a person power over others, which is part of the problem too. It's not only a matter of twisting Scripture.

MANIPULATING GOD

Satan is tempting Jesus to force the issue of safety on God, to put Him to the test. It would be like us saying, "Dear God, I am going to put myself knowingly and willingly in a bad situation, but I am going to ask You to bless me anyway." The Old Testament said that the Messiah would come, and would come to serve and save others. Satan is saying, "Hey, just forget about all of that now. Use Your power for Yourself! It will be fantastic. Everyone will gather around and surely follow." But to do that would abuse the position and go against Jesus's very identity.

Friends, don't deceive yourselves, for when you go to Scripture with that attitude, you're not looking for what you need to hear—you're looking for what you want to hear. It's another attempt at existing on your own terms. And we become what Rabbi Jonathan Sacks once said—when human beings try to become more than human, they quickly become less than human.

In the name of worshipping God, you're attempting to be God, but the place where you exist, solely on your own terms, apart from God forever, is actually called hell. Hell is saying, "God, I don't want Your beauty, I don't want Your truth, and I don't want Your goodness." You believe that if you stake everything on that and you follow that all the way out for the rest of your life, then God gives you what you want.

In the very short book of Third John, there is a fascinating reference to a man named Diotrephes. We hardly know anything about what he was doing, but the information given to us is telling. Apparently, he had a prominent position in the church, the religious outfit was on, and his position undoubtedly involved teaching and using Scripture. However, he had fallen into manipulating the community with malicious words. He was no longer serving God's purposes but instead sought to use God's church for his own purposes. The warning given concerning him can actually serve as a warning to us. John gets to the very heart of the matter when he tells us to beware of Diotrephes, who *loves to be first.*

Wait a minute—do I want to be first? Could that be a subtle temptation I'm giving in to as I look into my next opportunity? Such questions are healthy for you and me to ask. If our desire is simply to be first, then we can easily wrap ourselves in a religious facade, get our credentials, create unnecessary situations where people need to depend on us, all so that we can be seen and be needed. On the surface it may not look so obvious, but that is what makes religiosity so bad. We'll be celebrated on social media and even complimented in our communities for doing this. We'll be needed, liked, and in some cases, praised. Yet underneath, it's an attempt to manipulate the hand of God.

At this point, we might think, *Okay, given the human tendency to twist Scripture, the answer is to not take the Bible so seriously—look at what people can do with it!* But the answer, according to Jesus, is not to abandon the Scriptures but to cling more closely to them. It's there that we will find triumph over religious lies. Though the slave trade in the eighteen hundreds saw its fair share of leaders who twisted Scripture to support their position, it was actually a right view of Scripture that spearheaded a movement against it. William Wilberforce was used by God to manage a movement to abolish slavery, and the source he appealed to was the Word of God, handled rightly.

Imagine preaching the book of Leviticus, with its many laws on holiness and cleanness, and not point to Jesus! It would leave people with a giant burden of having to get themselves clean. Someone might say, "Well, at least it's a Bible study!" Maybe, but it's not a Christian Bible study. How can it be if you leave out Christ? All Scripture points toward and finds its ultimate fulfillment in Jesus.

It's the responsibility of the church to present Him as such. Knowing the Scriptures intellectually, however, is not enough to overcome religious temptations. We must respond to them.

When Jesus quotes Deuteronomy 6 against Satan's lies, He is teaching how to rightly handle the truth. We are never to come to God's Word with our own agenda but to look for God's will. Psalm 91, the passage Satan is quoting, does teach us about God's care, and yet the rest of Scripture also tells us that we are in no situation to demand it from God in the way we see fit. Scripture also tells us that there will be times of suffering. The whole picture is what we need. Am I looking at this text in light of the paragraph? Am I looking at this paragraph in light of the chapter? Am I looking at the chapter in light of the whole book? Am I looking at the book in light of Jesus? One way to guard against religious temptation is to saturate ourselves in a right handling of Scripture.

Knowing and handling the truth rightly is certainly the first step, but it's not the only step. Jesus overcomes not only by knowing the truth but yielding to the truth. It's through humble surrender to God that the lies of religion are defeated. Jesus did not climb up the ladder of self-centered glory; He came down in sacrificial service to accomplish God's purposes.

When temptation comes, especially in a religious package, here is what you need to do: Submit to God. Hear His Word and do it. This is so simple yet so powerful that Satan trembles. This is because we are dealing with a defeated Devil. We must yield to the truth that Scripture reveals, and we must view ourselves in light of what God wants for us, and act on it. When Satan tells us to go up, we are to come under the mighty hand of God. When we do that, the book of James tells us that the Devil will flee. It means that his power has been disarmed, for the way that he seeks to control you is through pride. Humility stops him in his tracks.

Satan's signature strategy should, at this point, be obvious to us. The special relationship between Father and Son is under attack. You will be most tempted toward religiosity when your relationship to God is in question. You will most likely be tempted toward religiosity when God's care and concern for you is called into question. *Does God* really *care for me? Does He* really *provide for me? Maybe I should put Him to the test?* These questions snake their way through our hearts and undermine the love that God has already proven. If Jesus had listened to Satan, God's whole redemption plan would have been brought into jeopardy. Instead, Jesus listened to His Father.

SURRENDER AS A WAY OF LIFE

In the garden of Gethsemane, hours before Jesus would be handed over to crucifixion, He wrestled with the pain that lay before Him. In prayer, He said, "My Father, if it be possible, let this cup pass from me; nevertheless, not as I will, but as you will" (Matt. 26:39). There would be a time Jesus would go to the holy city of Jerusalem, to be among the people and the crowds. But He would not go to save His own life; He would go for our sakes.

It was in the holy city that Jesus would be asked essentially the same question He was asked by Satan in Matthew 4. When He was on the cross—mocked, tortured, and humiliated—the people said, "If You are the Son of God, why don't You come down from that cross? Show us something spectacular! Show us a miracle and we will actually believe You!" The irony is, of course, that Jesus did indeed do the miraculous that day. He stayed to take the penalty for all our sins, so that we may be saved. His power was shown not by avoiding death but by going through it. The greatest example of proving His love was not by a spectacular show from the top of the holy temple, but by humble sacrifice on a Roman cross. On the surface, His surrender looked like defeat; in reality it was victory.

Religious lies tell us to grab positions by force, manipulate people, and take matters into our own hands, ignoring the reality of God's will. It's the temptation to be superspiritual. If these lies seem obvious, what is it that makes them so tempting to believe? Maybe, as Henri Nouwen suggests, it's that power offers an easy substitute for the hard task of love. It seems easier to be God than to love God, easier to control people than to love people, and easier to own life than to love life.[3] In other words, power is the preferred cultural substitute for love. Because our hearts are so quick at times to believe that God can't be trusted, that He will not care for us in the way we need, we think it's better to take control through religious performance because we can control the outcome. The remedy for our disposition to believe such lies is to look at the obedient surrender of Christ. When we look at the cross, these untruths are unmasked, for we see that God cares far more than we can imagine and He can be trusted more than we dared hope. As a result, our hearts are further transformed, demonstrating that the Christian life is not about religious manipulation but inside-out transformation. As we learn to trust Him from the heart, the need to wear the mask disintegrates and we discover a new kind of power, one that does not come from control but surrender.

But surrender isn't just a onetime thing; it's a lifestyle. Take the subway trains of the Los Angeles Metro, for example. (Yes, LA has a subway system. It doesn't go far, but it does exist.) As long as these electric train cars are connected to the third rail on the track, they have power. A car, on the other hand, needs fuel from a gas station before a long journey, and it eventually burns through its supply to the point of empty. When it comes to surrender, many of us are like cars; we get a little fuel from God in a church service, only to go our own way, making us vulnerable to temptation. But God wants us near and empowered not only for a moment but for a lifetime.[4] We should give ourselves to God daily, not waiting for the next church service or Christian event to do so. We are invited to be like the subway cars—always near and connected to the Source, to God Himself through Christ, not substituting relationship for religion.

Surrender will change everything about how you live your life. When lies are thrown your way, you recognize that you have a choice: to resist God or yield to Him. Temptation does not automatically draw you away; it can become your opportunity to draw nearer than you ever were before. Instead of testing God in those moments, trust Him. Draw close into a deeper, more intimate, and more obedient relationship with Him. And when we struggle to obey from the heart, let us look to the sacrifice of Christ. Seeing what He endured on our behalf truly melts our hearts, destroys our pride, and empowers us to humbly submit to His plans for us.

If God is truly the Source of life, love, and the power we need, then the wisest decision would be to depend on Him and yield to Him in obedience. That is why Salvation Army founder William Booth said, "The greatness of a man's power is the measure of his surrender."

The great temptation for me, as a leader, is to think that everything is fine as long as the religious ingredients are visible. Bible in hand? Check. Good attendance at church events? Check. But if these activities don't flow from a heart of surrender, they can give us a false sense of confidence. In fact, we can begin to feel as if we are justified by them, thinking that we wield some kind of personal power through our efforts. We may even be tempted to deliberately put ourselves in dangerous situations, demanding that God bless us. But the truth of the gospel tells a different story.

We cannot control God or prove ourselves to Him because of our sin. Spiritual disciplines such as Bible study and prayer are not ways of earning God's favor but enjoying God's favor. We don't need to throw ourselves down from a high religious tower in order to prove ourselves and test God. The gospel calls us to humble ourselves before Him, and He will lift us up in victory and we will experience true power. The only credentials we need are given to us through faith in Jesus. In Him we are declared as righteous. We are accepted by what He has done for us. Allow that truth to free you from playing a religious game and wearing a religious mask and you will walk strongly, overcoming the lies of Satan by drawing near to Jesus.

This is the way of surrender.

chapter seven

THE ART OF KILLING SIN

For if you live according to the flesh you will die, but if by the
Spirit you put to death the deeds of the body, you will live.

Romans 8:13

Im Dong-hyun, a South Korean archer, has only 20 percent vision in his left eye and 30 percent in his right, making him the most unlikely two-time gold-winning Olympic champion.[1] Although poor eyesight would seem a liability, for him it's an advantage. The blurred target becomes a blob of colors, making it easier for him to focus on his physical form, the wind, and the very reason he is competing in the first place. In South Korea, archery is more than recreation; it's an art that can win medals of honor for its people. Training can begin as early as nine years old and can include shooting up to one thousand arrows a day. Archers may perform in stadiums packed with spectators by day, and they may be shooting in demilitarized zones with soldiers by night. Whether in light or darkness, the archers' coaches tell them they are to remember their goal—to remember the country they belong to—for that is why they shoot. Apparently, for Im, it works. Though he sees only blurred colors when he peers toward his target more than seventy-five yards away, it doesn't stop him from hitting the grapefruit-sized center and smashing Olympic records.

I have talked with countless men and women who feel as though they simply have no choice when it comes to sin. Our old and fallen nature appears to condemn us to old and fallen patterns in life. When it comes to dealing with and overcoming sin in our lives, we are all the most unlikely candidates. And yet, recognizing this actually becomes our advantage. It becomes an invitation to focus on our new nature in Christ.

Whenever I'm speaking with a discouraged church member, or even to my own soul, I love to read what Paul writes in Romans 8, that though sin is *possible*, it's no longer *inevitable*. Well aware of the weakness of our "flesh," as the apostle Paul calls it, we can learn to depend more on the Spirit's power. Being born-again means that we are no longer obligated to the demands of the sinful nature—in fact we are at war with it.

Kill sin or sin will kill you, the saying goes. When it comes to the battlefield of the soul, we are not shooting arrows at a practice target. We have a real Enemy. This reality should lead us to focus on Christ, leaning into Him and learning to kill off whatever is against Him within our hearts. There can be no conversation about overcoming temptation without also talking about killing sin. And there can be no talk about killing sin unless we remember who we belong to.

REMEMBER WHO YOU ARE

Many religions in the world talk about how one must fight against the evils of the world, but what about the evil within? This is precisely what Paul the apostle says we must do if we are to follow Christ and become who God has declared us to be. He has already told us that when we believe, we are united with Christ and have His Spirit dwelling in us. He has given us a new heart, new desires, and new power. Therefore, to be at home with Jesus is to be at odds with whatever is against Him. As followers of Jesus Christ, we have not only new power but new obligations. When Paul was writing about our identity in Christ and our obligations to Him, he had very practical implications in mind.

You are on your way to becoming glorious in God; His power and presence have given you everything necessary to get there. In the meantime, there are things we must do as evidences of this power working in us. You have a new obligation … to do what? To "put to death the deeds of the body" or, as the old translations say, "mortify the flesh."

I must admit, I love the word "mortify." The way we use the word today doesn't quite carry the weight that it did back in the day. If you show up to a party wearing the same outfit as another person (classic LA problem), you might say, "OH. MY. GOODNESS. I was mortified!" In the seventeenth century, however, it was a radical word. John Owen, the Puritan writer, used it in the title of his book that today sounds like a great album: *The Mortification of Sin*. "To mortify" actually means "to kill." There is a violence to the Christian life, but it's not with other people or other nations. It's a war with sinful desires within our own selves.

Let's face it, everyone gets nervous when anyone remotely religious uses the word "war." Between culture wars and holy wars, there is enough historical baggage to make anyone nervous. Why use violent terms to describe the Christian life? Isn't there enough violence in the world today? But what we must understand is that the reason we see war in our nation and in the world today is because violence is not taking place against sin. The reason we see so much evil today is because sin is not being killed. The reason that some of us are struggling and are feeling defeated may be due in part to our failure to kill sin. This may sound like a strange endeavor, but it's absolutely necessary in following Jesus.

The more radical we are with our sin, the more free we become. I don't want any of this to remain theoretical—I want us to think very practically and simply about what it means to kill sin. Let me frame it in five steps.

1. KNOW YOUR TARGET

What did Paul mean when he said we should "put to death the deeds of the body"? He is referring to all actions of life influenced by sin. The body, or the deeds that we do with it, when influenced by sin, becomes an instrument of sin. Each outward act has an inward origin. That is why Jesus said, "But what comes out of the mouth proceeds from the heart, and this defiles a person. For out of the heart come evil thoughts, murder, adultery, sexual immorality, theft, false witness, slander" (Matt. 15:18–19). The desire grabs hold of your body and says, "This will work!" We must kill it off at the source and spot it within our own hearts.

There was a woman I met in church who was all about ministry. Having come out of a particularly crazy and dark background, she took every opportunity she could to serve and lead. Her ministry began with Sunday morning service opportunities, continued through involvement in church ministry teams, and then expanded to leading what we call in our church "community groups." That's when it all went weird. As she later admitted, she would gossip about other leaders in order to gain the loyalty of those within the group. Noticing some manipulative trends in her leadership, fellow leaders called her out on it. It wasn't received well. She was freaked out that anyone dare question her leadership; didn't they realize that she *needed* to lead? That was the heart of the problem. After some time she became aware that it was not the Spirit who was driving her into leadership; it was her need to be in control. Had this target been identified earlier on, it would have saved her—and others—a lot of harm.

Too many Christians think that as long as they don't live in overtly sinful environments, they can be relatively sin-free. This is a lie. We saw in the wilderness temptation of Jesus that He was tempted by Satan, not necessarily with *bad* things but by *bad* motivations. I cannot stress how important this is. You can do all kinds of good deeds but with sinful desires. If you want to get rid of spiderwebs in your house, first get rid of the spider.

Depending on your Christian background, you might find all this focus on evil desires somewhat unnecessary. I often hear it from people in my own church: "The sinful nature doesn't reign over us anymore! Why talk about it?" Here's why. Though sin may not preside over us, it still resides within us. If you are unaware of this, you may unknowingly come under its control. We must know our enemy and identify our target. Though we are indeed on our way to glory, we must be aware of indwelling sin. It won't be completely gone until we are resurrected.

2. KNOW YOUR PATTERNS

Though every person has a sin nature, it's not always expressed in the same ways because we all have varied inclinations that have created different patterns in our lives. It may look different for everybody. Like archers learning to shoot well, we need to identify and unlearn habits that would distract us from our goal. Learning the art of killing sin is recognizing what we are prone to, and one way that we can discern this is by taking a look into the past.

Though my brother and I grew up in the same house and within the same general culture, our temptations toward evil could not have been more different. My brother would smoke weed, drink beer, and get angry. He would pick fights with anyone and everyone, just to get his aggression out. You did not want to be in his path when he saw red.

Me on the other hand? I liked to PAR-TAY. I wanted to have fun. When I would take LSD or drink, it was because I wanted to escape. Before I became a Christian, I was also very sexually promiscuous, thinking it would meet my need for validation and escape.

Thank goodness, God saved both my brother and me. We are new creatures in Christ, and we both happen to be pastors. Like every other Christian, we still have our sin nature, but what tempts us looks different. Our old patterns make us more alert to present temptations. Take films, for example. Because my brother struggled with anger and rage, he avoids watching movies that contain violence; it's just a temptation for him and he knows it. For me, it looks different. A film with violence doesn't appeal to me, but one full of hedonistic escapism would be like poison. Now, think of the implications this has for someone like me in ministry. Because old patterns lead me toward escapism, one particular temptation for me today would be to say yes to every ministry opportunity outside of my church, the easy faraway stuff. This would relieve me of the difficulties of doing real life together as a church, week after week, in both the good times and bad.

You need to recognize your own inclinations. Satan will come with tailor-made temptations, seeking to capitalize on your areas of weakness. It's crucial that we know our Enemy's tactics. Confess these to close friends and more importantly before the Lord. It's part of winning the war. But it doesn't stop there.

3. AIM WELL, SHOOT TRUE

You have probably heard the phrase "Just give it to God!" numerous times in church, and it's often said in relation to sin. Part of this is true. We need to "give it to God" in the sense that we need forgiveness and strength to overcome. But God also gives us responsibility; we must make choices. We are not to just sit there and wait passively because we've been given the power of the Spirit and the instruction of God's Word to put sin to death.

Before he was known as one of the great theologians of the early church, Augustine had a lust problem. If you read his story, you will find it has such a modern ring to it. He was a man who could not resist sexual temptation and even had a child out of wedlock. In his famous *Confessions* he describes himself at a time in his life when he was aware of it and of its badness, and yet also his unwillingness to let it go in a period of his life. His prayer was, as ours often are, "Lord, give me purity … but not yet."

But sinful desires don't die automatically. We have a responsibility to kill them off. I've talked with many people who feel stuck in their sin. They say, "I don't know what to do. I've received advice and counsel from so many others, but nothing changes." I ask, "Have you made choices based on their counsel? Have you actually decided for yourself?" Because no one else can kill your sin; it's your responsibility. Unfortunately, my wife cannot mortify the sin in my heart, and neither can my children nor my friends in the church. It's the Holy Spirit in me that enables me to put sin to death. If you don't realize this, you will become a frustrated and bitter person, blaming others, perhaps even blaming the church, when all the while the person you have become is shaped by your unwillingness to kill your own sin.

I think all of us would just love to get "zapped" by God and never struggle with sin again. *If I can just go to this special conference or service and get zapped, I will never struggle with sin again!* But it doesn't happen like that. It's a learning process, shaping the type of people we become along the way.

When Jesus said, "If your right hand causes you to sin, cut it off" (Matt. 5:30), He was making an intentional overstatement in order to get a point across. It certainly does the job. To kill sin is to take away its strength, to cut off its supply. There are certain influences that subtly feed our sinful inclinations. Take the film example again. If you struggle with overdesire for romance, then watching the same romantic comedy one hundred times will probably be toxic. Though watching the film itself is not a sin, it can be a weakening influence in your life, a supply line that feeds the flesh. Don't misunderstand me; I'm not saying that we blame films for all our problems but rather our sinful inclinations that can be fed by them. It means coming to God and saying, "Lord, You know my overdesires, my wrong desires, and You know I am inclined in the direction of _____. I recognize this and ask for Your help in choosing what is helpful and healthy for my life." That is getting to the supply line. You kill the fruit of sin by killing the root of sin.

4. DON'T GET DISTRACTED

Sin can have this hypnotizing effect on us. If we allow it to grow, it turns our eyes from our true focus, and we become blind to the effect it's having in our lives. John Owen captures this well when he tells us that sin will "darken the mind, extinguish convictions, dethrone reason, interrupt the power and influence of any considerations that may be brought to hamper it, and break through all into a flame."[2] When our sin is clearly in view, we must not become distracted—we must act on conviction.

Don't make peace with sin. It's easy to do. We may be very well aware of a particular sin and understand that it is bad and that it must go. God has convicted you, and yet you let it live. You may, as I have in times past, even pray like this: "Dear God, I want to obey in all these areas … but, please, just let this little sin live."

When you read the story of the kings in the Old Testament, you might be tempted to write them off and throw them under the bus, assuming you are nothing like them. However, our requests of God are often very similar. Many of those kings fell into wickedness because they did not act on the conviction that God brings. The more they resisted, the further they moved from God and became known as wicked. Kings like Saul had many chances to listen to the conviction of God but continued to be distracted by ego. One of the reasons Saul became the paranoid jealous king was because he chose to make peace with his sin, not with his God.

Imagine being merciful to something like cancer; ridiculous, right? That is how it sounds to God when we ask Him to allow sin to continue. We must be careful that when asking God for mercy, we don't mean asking for God's tolerance. Quoting John Owen once more: "Do you think he will ease you of that which perplexes you, that you may be at liberty to that which no less grieves him?"[3] Make no mistake, sin is always an enemy, never a friend.

5. KEEP ON SHOOTING

Here is a sobering truth: you could walk with Jesus for years and years, and yet the minute you begin to relax on sin is the moment you are in a dangerous position. Sin seems friendly, harmless. Perhaps it's been so long that a particular temptation doesn't seem so bad. That is exactly what Satan wants, to dull our sensitivity to sin, hoping we will give up the fight.

Recently, in a period of about twenty-four hours, I heard reports of three ministers I knew who had fallen from grace. It was shocking. It reminded me of how fragile we are and how desperately we must cling to Christ. I received a call from a dear pastor friend of mine when the news came out about these scandals, and while we were processing together on the phone, he read a quote to me. It freaked me out. I kind of want you to be freaked out as well, in a healthy way, of course. Dr. Howard Hendricks said, "Satan will lie in the weeds for forty years to entrap one of God's servants. He is patient. He will wait and he will watch for just the right moment. A moment that will do greater damage to the kingdom of God."

I have known and observed Christians for many years who I never would have suspected as candidates for scandal or moral failure. And yet, it happens more than I like to admit. Because of such stories, the word *evangelical* has become synonymous with *scandal*, at least in my city. But this does not have to be the case for us. We must be vigilant, watchful, and mindful that our Enemy, the Devil, is like a lion seeking someone to devour. Let's not give him the pleasure.

My biggest concern for the people in my church is not necessarily for those who are dealing with sin; it's for those who don't realize that there is a need to deal with it at all! Self-sufficiency and prayerlessness reveal a loss of intimacy with God, and a hardness develops. Their downfall tends to begin with self-sufficiency and prayerlessness. This is what makes you comfortable with sin. Owen describes it like this: "You that were tender, and used to melt under the word, under afflictions, will grow as some have profanely spoken, 'sermon-proof.'"[4] He is talking about our ability to rally our inner lawyers to come to our defense. We pretend that what the preacher said on Sunday, what we read in our Bibles that morning, or what a friend warned us about in a text doesn't apply to us.

Hopefully, as Peter did on the night he betrayed his Lord and friend, we melt at the glance of Jesus. Conviction is like a spiritual smelling salt that Christ uses to wake us up.

OF DUTY AND DELIGHT

In cities such as LA, you learn to make the most out of the small property space you have, perhaps building a little planter box for an urban garden. I have no green thumb. In fact, I don't really know what that even means, but I do know one thing about our precious little garden: the weeds have to go. It's the beauty and joy of the garden itself, not my hatred of weeds, that drives me to rip out what threatens to kill it. The same is true in the Christian life: it's the beauty of God's love for you in Christ that fuels you to deal radically with anything that would threaten it.

There are wrong ways to kill sin. You can't tell people who do not have Christ to mortify their sin, because they have no weapons, no ammo! This is where much of Christian history has gone wrong. Followers of Jesus, forgetting the very message they believed that gave them new life, tell nonbelievers to stop being sinful. Maybe this is why so many people think Christianity is only about being a good person.

You have heard, I'm sure, of the fruit-tree metaphor to describe the difference between gospel Christianity and religiosity. A person trying to "make themselves good," a religious person, is like someone gluing apples to a dead tree. It's only a superficial surface-level change. Now, this does not mean that we should preach against sin, for this is how we come under conviction. But the only solution for our sins and the only power to fight them in daily life comes from Jesus Himself. There is no death to sin without the death of Christ. He makes the tree good and produces fruit through us. This, the Bible calls, is the doctrine of justification. It's what makes Christianity so gloriously different from all other religions. There is new life, new power, new desires, new ability! When Paul says mortify sin by the Spirit, he is referring to this true power Source that lies within you to kill sin.

You are not on your own. And though we need to hear warnings, we are not to live in fear. The responsibility to kill sin means that we are not secure in our salvation; it's actually the reverse. The responsibility to kill is the fruit of our salvation. This is what we need to take to heart as we face daily temptation.

On the one hand, killing sin is a necessity, not an option. It's the evidence that we truly are born-again and changed by Jesus. But on the other hand, we must clearly state that killing sin is the result of our justification, not the cause of it. Jesus never tells us to get our act together on our own, then come to Him when we have done so. That is not the message of the gospel. Rather, through faith in Him we are made right before God and receive new power for a new life on our way to glory. That which condemned me, that which dragged me to death, that which dragged me into condemnation, I will be a part of no more. And, by the Spirit, they will be removed. This means that facing temptation and killing sin can actually be done with joy.

Isn't that masochism? No. It's the kind of joy you have when you are tending a garden, removing the weeds that kill in order for fruit to thrive. Our life is like a garden, and the Divine Gardener has come into our lives to bring forth incredible fruit, and this means killing off that which kills. Each time we put sin to death, we do so in pursuit of life. Overcoming temptation is not the ultimate goal; it is a necessary part of the journey on our way to the goal of becoming more like Christ.

chapter eight

WHEN SUCCESS LIES

*Again, the devil took him to a very high mountain and showed
him all the kingdoms of the world and their glory. And he said to
him, "All these I will give you, if you will fall down and worship me."
Then Jesus said to him, "Be gone, Satan! For it is written, 'You
shall worship the Lord your God and him only shall you serve.'"*

Matthew 4:8–10

George Mallory was one of the first to ever climb Mount Everest, and when he was asked why, he answered famously, "Because it was there."[1] For him the challenge of the mountain portrayed the upward struggle of life, one he describes climbing with sheer joy. He told his wife he wanted to prove worthy of her by his work. But years later, his son wrote these piercing words: "I would so much rather have known my father than to have grown up in the shadow of a legend, a hero, as some people perceive him to be."[2] When author Zack Eswine writes about this story, he asks this question: "So why did George choose to engage the challenges of the mountain but not the living room?"[3] The perception of George Mallory in the public eye was "hero," but his son simply wanted a father. Mallory had a version of success that involved climbing a mountain, but could it have also included raising a son?

There's nothing necessarily wrong with climbing mountains, but the question is, at what cost? A story such as this one invites me to ask not only what I truly value in life but why I value it in the first place. One conversation with my relatives revealed that depending on how we were all raised, our views on what we value may differ greatly. Have a talk with your parents, chat with their parents, watch a little History Channel and you will quickly find that people have defined success differently throughout the ages. So differently, in fact, that it might even shock us.

In Greco-Roman society the aspiration of many young boys was to become a Spartan, a killing machine of the ancient world.[4] In those days status was not always connected to cash and commerce—those were necessary evils. But acts of glory brought through battle? Marvelous. I can't imagine having a son running to me saying, "When I grow up, I want to kill enemies and make no money!" I would be more than a little frightened. Move forward in time and success was defined by your rank in high society. Think *Pride and Prejudice* with a little *Downton Abbey* thrown in. Living the dream in the Victorian age meant being a "duke" or a "duchess," a landowner with great influence. You certainly wouldn't be slaying people or hunting them down, although you might have a duel that consisted of smacking each other with handkerchiefs. Wealth was key, and a place in an influential family gave you power. It was a different take on status than the centuries before.

What is our version of success? Does it consist of entrepreneurial start-ups? Education from an Ivy League college? Climbing the highest mountain? If our version of success is already developed in our minds, we must ask where it came from in the first place. However you define success determines how you live your life. Scripture tells us that there are all kinds of different influences shaping us, forming how we view a successful life. Some of them can be good and healthy, while others can be destructive. Jesus, through His life and teachings, shows us what these destructive versions are and how to resist them.

In the wilderness temptations, we see Satan as a dealer in lies about our basic needs and tempting us toward religious hypocrisy. But if these don't work, he will sell you a success story. The problem is, he has left truth out of the script. If the first temptation in the wilderness was to be sub-Christian, and the second to be super-Christian, this last temptation is for us to become semi-Christian. It's perhaps one of the most powerful lies of all. And it's not hard to see why.

LEGITIMATE GOALS

In this final temptation, Jesus is taken to a high mountain and shown the kingdoms of the world and their glory. I suppose in our time it would be like seeing a giant advertisement of New York, London, and Paris, and all their landmarks at the same time. We might immediately assume that what's on offer is outright wrong, as if we should just make a mental note saying, *Don't desire the kingdoms of the world … Got it*. But it's not that simple. The kingdoms of the world contain people. Is this a bad goal? Is it wrong to pursue people? Isn't that why Jesus came into our world? Yes it is. The kingdoms of the world are not, in and of themselves, a bad goal. Many of our goals in life—to do a good job at work, pursue art or business, or raise a family—are not inherently evil. So when does a definition of success become satanic? When *legitimate* goals are viewed and pursued in *illegitimate* ways.

It's funny, as a Christian, I hear and talk about sacrificial service all the time. I know it's a virtue to be pursued. Yet how often does that play out in my plans? I'll be honest, when I get my paycheck, self-sacrifice is not the first thing that naturally comes to mind. It's very tempting to willingly climb on top of others, excuse greedy motives, and basically sanctify selfish ambition in the name of success. Of course, it can just as easily happen in the church as well. Christian organizations can employ underhanded business practices all in the name of "getting good resources out there." A church leader can launch plans driven by ego, building their own kingdom, as long as it's done in "Jesus's name." Ouch.

There is a principle running through all three temptations of Matthew 4 that Satan uses against Jesus and uses against us. It's the principle of self-service, not self-sacrifice. "Do everything for yourself," the Devil whispers in our ears. "You have power. Why not use it for yourself?" This attitude governs much of our thinking in daily life. "Who cares if others get pushed down along the way?" we tell ourselves. "How else am I going to be successful?" One offer to Jesus in the wilderness is the option of pursuing His mission without self-sacrifice. Satan is essentially saying, "You came to this planet for the kingdoms of the world, right? Well, I have a way You can get them without that whole self-sacrifice part, without that whole suffering thing. I can give You what You see on the mountain without the cross." Legitimate goals, illegitimate ways.

CAPTURING OUR IMAGINATIONS

There are two ways, I think, that Satan tries to keep God out of the picture. One way is to keep us from the Bible entirely. If we are ignorant of the truth, then we won't walk in the truth. But if that fails, there is a second strategy. Bombard us with so much information and so many options that we are overwhelmed and don't even know what to do with it all. The voice of God becomes drowned out by a thousand other voices. The *New York Times* has published studies that show that the average consumer is bombarded with five thousand advertisements per day.[5] If this is true, then we are literally swimming among messages designed to create desire and supply ready-made solutions. They shape our idea of success. Satan would gladly have us pursue goals that seem so normal and feel so natural that we don't even feel the need to consult God or consider Him in the equation.

In this case, it doesn't really matter what the thing is that we are pursuing because, as we lose sight of God in the process, Satan views it as a win for his team. Dietrich Bonhoeffer, Christian pastor and martyr in Nazi-era Germany, spoke of this in his writings—that it makes no difference whether the temptation appeals to sexual desire, self-centered ambition, desire for revenge, love of fame and power, or greed for money. What matters, he says, is that in the moment of temptation "God is quite unreal to us, he loses all reality … Satan does not here fill us with hatred of God, but with forgetfulness of God."[6] Falling deep into temptation can be as simple as forgetting God in our life script.

Call it a daydream, that story of success that plays again and again on the cinema screen of our imaginations. It's our envisioning how our lives are going to look in the future and what we need to do in order to get there. Satan would love to capitalize on this and provide a smooth path to our dream goals. There is only one problem. God and His ways are not included. The Devil is constantly trying to sell us a success story in which God is absent or optional. When our own ambition has made God a mere stagehand in the success story, we have bought into a lie. It will turn out to be only a cautionary tale.

There is no mountaintop nearly high enough to afford a view of the global glory described, yet we are told that Jesus was *shown* the kingdoms of the world. We assume it must have been some kind of vision Satan is broadcasting, trying to capture the imagination of Jesus. He doesn't simply come up to Jesus and say, "Hey, I really think it's about time You worshipped me. I've got some random stuff here that might convince You." No, he is appealing to the very thing Jesus Himself is after. To get it, however, is going to require pushing God aside and worshipping a substitute instead. It's going to cost.

YOUR ALLEGIANCE

"All of these will be Yours," the tempter says to Jesus, "if You will bow down and worship me."

Really? Devil worship? The very phrase conjures up images of B-grade horror flicks in which neighborhood cats are sacrificed to the sound track of eighties heavy metal. Most temptation, however, involves nothing of the sort (though I'm sure it happens in Hollywood all the time). But although hilarious images such as these are easy to dismiss, make no mistake, Jesus understands this temptation as having everything to do with worship.

When we ascribe to a person, position, or possession of ultimate value, we are pledging our allegiance. We are, in fact, worshipping. We worship by sacrificing lesser things in our pursuit of what we believe to be the greatest thing. The Enemy's goal is to get us to desire something so greatly that we will take it … with or without God. It controls your life because it has your allegiance. If anything in this life becomes more important than God, it has become an idol and you play into the hands of the Enemy. The moment you are willing to do absolutely *anything* in order to succeed in your vocation, your social circles, or even your church is the moment you have made it a god.

Jesus understands with crystal clarity what is going on in Satan's offer, and it's made clear by the passage of Scripture that Jesus quotes in response. In Deuteronomy 6, God told Israel in the wilderness that they were not to have any other gods before Him; this was the very first of the Ten Commandments. Satan's offers to us are always an attempt to get us to break it. It's a temptation toward idolatry, to live out an alternative story of success, where God takes a backseat. The cost is our allegiance.

I read recently in the news about a mom in Pennsylvania who wanted her children to succeed in school so badly that she committed three crimes. The kids were not doing as well as she thought they should—the grades they had received for their work were not to her standards. In desperation, she broke into the school computer system. She had previously worked for the school district and was skilled in using the system. Since her departure, however, she had been locked out of the system. But she was driven, and she successfully hacked her way into the database and manually changed her children's grades. She even saw the need to change one of her kids' grades from a 98 percent to 99. She was caught and charged. What was her motive? Idolatry. She wanted a version of success so badly she was willing to break the law to get it.

Some of us hear that story and think, *Wow, that was totally my mom.* Others would say, "That doesn't sound like a temptation to me at all." For you it might look different. But remember this, her decision to place her kids on a pedestal came long before she learned her computer-hacking skills. Lest we dismiss her case too quickly, in what area of your life are you most tempted to place something above God? Or, let me put it in a different way, a more personal way: What lie are you most tempted to believe? Whatever that is, you will sacrifice for it. It's how we worship. Don't misunderstand me; we should be passionate about what we do. It's good and right to want to work hard, use our talents, and be an influence in the culture! But the minute we love it more than God, our allegiance has changed and we ruin ourselves. In the end, it will cost us our souls.

COUNTING THE COST

The temptation is to believe a success story in which God is optional. The temptation can be subtle. It's to love something so much that you are willing to do absolutely anything to get it, even if it means worshipping something other than God. What we must understand, however, is that this is rarely a onetime decision.

The success story that Satan sells is built on a lie. Though he may promise everything, the Bible tells us that he has only the power to destroy, not to deliver. The reason that believing these lies and building on them costs you your soul is that you slowly become like the one who presented you the plan, because whatever you worship, you become like. Jesus once said, "What will it profit a man if he gains the whole world and forfeits his soul?" (Matt. 16:26). What do you have when you build your life on a lie? Destruction.

Temptation is not a once-in-a-lifetime thing. Wouldn't it be nice if it were? If temptation were like going to get your driver's license? Just show up to the spiritual DMV and say to the clerk, "Hi, I just turned sixteen. I'm here to defeat Satan once and for all. Do you have an open appointment?" No, temptation is something we must endure every day. In fact, when the gospel of Luke recounts the wilderness temptation for us, he includes this little reminder: "And when the devil had ended every temptation, he departed from him until an opportune time" (4:13). That's interesting. Sobering, even. It means that there will be moments when we are more vulnerable than others, so we must be aware. Because this particular brand of temptation has to do with success, we can expect it to come at times in our lives when things are going according to plan. There will be seasons when life will be hard and things won't be working out as we thought they should. In these times, lies will abound, and they will be easier to believe. In order to defeat them, we must know what they cost.

Knowing that temptation is a daily battle, we can easily become overwhelmed. But it's there in those moments of desperation that we find the greatest deliverance. What does that look like?

THE WAY OF ESCAPE

Of the many Scripture passages on temptation, 1 Corinthians 10:13 is perhaps the most familiar. It also happens to be incredibly practical. Paul writes, "No temptation has overtaken you that is not common to man. God is faithful, and he will not let you be tempted beyond your ability, but with temptation he will also provide the way of escape, that you may be able to endure it." In the midst of temptation, we have an opportunity to move in the direction of God and act on our true identity as His children. This way out also happens to be the way up.

You are not alone. This is the first thing you need to know. Our tendency is to think that no one has ever experienced what we have. Some of you might even say to yourselves, *Nobody knows what it's like to be tempted the way that I am. You can't even imagine the kind of temptation I face!* Nothing could be further from the truth. At the heart of the matter, we all experience the same essence of temptation, though the form may look different. We can find encouragement in community if we would confess our struggles to one another.

You will not be tempted beyond your ability. Secondly, Paul says that you will never find yourself in a situation in which the only possible choice is to do evil. There will never be a time when you can say, "Well, the only choice I had was to steal/fornicate/abuse/lie!" There will always be a righteous option in every situation. It may not be easy. In fact, it may be the very hardest option to choose, but you will always have a choice in temptation. Satan can never take that away from you.

There will always be a way of escape. Lastly, we are told by Paul that there will always be a way of escape. It's a wonderful truth! The question is, how do we choose it? Clearly it's not as simple as a little red box that says, "In case of temptation, break glass." How do we choose that way of escape? The following verse gives us a clue. It says, "Therefore, my beloved, flee from idolatry" (1 Cor. 10:14). Here is a key truth we must understand about temptation in order to endure it: If we think that temptation is only something "out and over there," seeking to make its way into our lives, we will always be powerless to defeat it. Because that is actually not the whole picture about temptation. When we understand that the desire for what is tempting us comes from within, we are then on our way to overcoming. That is why Paul, in the context of temptation, says, "Flee from idolatry."

How do we take this way of escape, practically? First of all, talk to God about your temptation. Name it, call it what it is in His presence through prayer. I find such freedom in just being brutally honest about what is tempting me. *God, I'm super jealous of that person, and I kind of want something bad to happen to him [or her] … Help me see both him [or her] and myself in light of Your grace.* Liberating, isn't it? See, one of the reasons we don't cash in on this promise of escape is because we are unwilling to speak with God about what exactly is tempting us. Then secondly, avoid situations that will be particularly tempting for you. Now, I have been making the point throughout this whole book that temptation is everywhere, and indeed it is. But let's face it, some situations and environments are more tempting than others. If you find yourself in one of these, leave—don't add fuel to the fire. And thirdly, invite others into your lives and give them permission to help you in moments of weakness. The more we take these steps, the more freedom we will experience.

REFUSAL BY LOVE

In order to endure and overcome temptation, we must recognize that the whole reason we are tempted is because we are being drawn by our own desires to want something above God. Temptation would have no power if there were not desire within. This means *overcoming temptation has to do with a reordering of desire that reshapes our character*. It's not enough to just not want the lying success story; you need to want something else more.

Classic pastor illustration: There is a couple that drives their car to the service station. The husband, sitting behind the wheel, asks the attendant to clean the windshield. The attendant cleans the windshield and walks over to the window to receive payment. "The window is still filthy!" the husband cries. "You need to clean it again." The wife looks to the husband and says, "Honey, look at me." The husband turns toward her. She takes off his glasses, wipes them, and puts them back on. The windshield is spotless.

We are so used to looking at our lives through distorted lenses that all these versions of success blur our vision for what we think we need in life. Jesus, with the clarity and power of the truth, cleans our glasses, as it were, so that we might see what we should really be living for.

God is the Source of all that is good, true, and beautiful. Satan never created a thing; he can only blur and distort. Only in God will we find a version of success that doesn't end in destruction but life!

For His story is the story of redemption, of His kingdom coming to earth, healing our brokenness, and making all things new! Part of overcoming the temptation to elevate lesser things above God is in recognizing them to be, well, lesser! C. S. Lewis put it simply, and brilliantly:

> Indeed, if we consider the unblushing promises of reward and the staggering nature of the rewards promised in the Gospels, it would seem that Our Lord finds our desires not too strong, but too weak. We are half-hearted creatures, fooling about with drink and sex and ambition when infinite joy is offered us, like an ignorant child who wants to go on making mud pies in a slum because he cannot imagine what is meant by the offer of a holiday at the sea. We are far too easily pleased.[7]

The movie that should be playing on the cinema screens of our imaginations should be the realities and glories of God and His redemptive work. This was the case with Jesus in the wilderness, where His mind was saturated with the Word of God in all its truths and all its excellencies, and His refusal to Satan was rooted in His affection for His Father. If we would look and see this beauty, our hearts would melt! Our affections for the true and living God would move us to say no to all the counterfeits.

"Be gone …," Jesus says to Satan. "For it is written, 'You shall worship the Lord your God and him only shall you serve.'" Here we learn to overcome the lying success, following Christ as our model and trusting Him as our Savior. Again and again we see Jesus immersed in Scripture, evidenced by the fact that He responds to every temptation with Scripture. To paraphrase, Jesus is saying, "Satan, you are selling Me a script that doesn't involve the cross, and I am refusing you because I know what lies behind your temptation." Jesus's vision of success was determined by loving God and loving people. He would go after the people of the world, but not in Satan's ways or for Satan's reasons.

Jesus refused Satan because His allegiance already lay elsewhere. The key to overcoming temptation is a heart captivated by God. As Christ was focused on the plan ahead of Him to rescue lives, we must focus on the fact that God has involved us in His work. He has a greater purpose for our gifts, talents, and abilities than we could ever imagine. They are not small and self-centered; they are huge and kingdom-minded!

Jesus is our example, and we follow that by soaking up Scripture for ourselves. Not only as individuals but as a community! As we do, we can look at our circumstances, jobs, and relationships through the lens of God's truth. Satan comes along and tries to sell you a counterfeit story. You refuse because you already have a glorious gospel story blazing bright on the screen in your heart!

My kids are probably annoyed with it now, but when we watch a film for Family Movie Night (yes, it's a thing in my house), I love to show how the grand themes of the story can only be fulfilled in the gospel. The villains remind us of our need for forgiveness and transformation, the protagonists speak to our need for mission and meaning, the problems and trials in the plot remind us of our need for redemption and hope, and the sacrifice of one character for another points us beyond man-made stories to the ultimate sacrifice of Christ! "We KNOW, Dad …" is the usual response from my kids these days, but I do hope they never forget.

May we never forget.

If there is indeed a God and ultimate reality beneath and behind it all, then we must use our gifts and abilities to help point to this ultimate story. JRR Tolkien, like many other writers, believed that God gives gifts and talents, such as writing, for this very purpose. To point toward ultimate meaning in God's world. This is why, whether through books or films, narrative is so powerful. Looking at the world through the lens of the gospel keeps us alert and awake to the great themes of the grand story of Christ.

The key in overcoming temptation is not simply to "be a good little Christian and read the Bible." The key is to understand it, soak in it, and look at the Word through it. When you see that God is the ultimate plot fulfillment of this giant story called humanity, you will be captivated.

The first commandment is that we should love God above all. In fact, you never break any of the other commandments without having broken the first one. The reverse is also true. It's as we love God that we live life the way He intends. The command to worship God is also the invitation to be satisfied in God. God wouldn't command you to worship Him above everything else if He was not the highest and greatest good for humanity. Find your satisfaction in Him. From that place we are empowered to overcome the lies.

Now let's be honest. We don't always do this. It's not enough to just try to follow Jesus as our example. We have all failed in temptation, which is why you must know that it's only through trusting

Christ as Savior that you can truly overcome and refuse the lying success of Satan. Jesus didn't just come to be our example. He came to be our Savior. He rejected the easy path shown to Him by Satan on the mountain, and He chose the hard path of another mountain, one that had a cross.

Because His goal was to come and save us, to die for our sins, to pay the penalty for where we have failed and committed idolatry. Because He did not give in, He is able to save those who have given in. He endured temptation to save people who didn't. Jesus did not resist temptation in order to condemn you for giving in to yours. He resisted temptation in order to save you. He provides not only a way of escape from giving in but also forgiveness for when we do.

In all temptation there are two kingdoms, and they're vying for your allegiance. Satan says, "Give me your life." Christ says, "I have given you Mine." Which one will you follow?

When you place God above all else, though it comes with great sacrifice, all the things that we truly need are added to us. And you can face whatever Satan brings with a simple, "No. You're done." Because Jesus refused to take the easy path and instead gave everything for you.

Give Him your all. He gave His all for you. That's how we overcome.

chapter nine

THE HOPE IN OUR TRIAL

Then those who had seized Jesus led him to Caiaphas the high
priest, where the scribes and the elders had gathered. And Peter
was following him at a distance, as far as the courtyard of the high
priest, and going inside he sat with the guards to see the end.

Matthew 26:57–58

Life often comes with a microphone. During the 2011 British general election, Gordon Brown, the prime minister at that time, got in his car after speaking with a woman about foreign workers in the United Kingdom. And then he ruined his chance for reelection. Forgetting that his microphone from the television interview was still on, he began complaining to his aides about such a bigoted woman.[1] His remarks were broadcast immediately, and no amount of apologies could rescue the situation. The moment he realized he was on trial, the verdict was already in.

Though we have been talking about temptation and particular times of testing, the truth is that we are always on trial—if not in the courtroom, then in the courtyard of daily life. Perhaps many of us feel this way already—in our jobs, with our looks, in our social circles. But we have been talking about something deeper than what appears on the surface such as talent or image. We are talking about our nature. Even what others don't see, God sees. He brings it to light. Like the crisis of the South Korean ferry or King David's midnight stroll near Bathsheba's house or the microphone on the prime minister, trials don't *create* what is within us; trials *reveal* what is within us.

The mic is on. It's only a matter of whether we realize it and how we respond when we do. This scene takes our conversation about choices, temptation, and character from the private sphere out into the public square, where we are always on trial. But the truths of this text teach us how to face it without fear.

There are few places in which this truth is revealed more dramatically or poetically than in the narrative of Christ's last night before His death on the cross. We have seen Jesus privately tested in the wilderness, but here we see Him publicly tested in the city. In the wilderness, the crowds were gone and Satan's temptations were up front, but in this story the crowd is present and Satan moves to the background, much like our daily experience with temptation. But scholar and commentator Frederick Dale Bruner points out that when Matthew records the midnight trial of the Messiah, he is actually recording two trials at once. One is official, revealing the truth about Jesus, His identity, and His faithfulness. The second trial is unofficial, revealing the truth about the crowd—particularly Judas, the religious leaders, and the man named Peter. Everyone in the crowd faces temptation within the trial, but only Peter is transformed through it. Why? What is it that we learn in this trial that will transform us through our trial? The moving moments of this trial teach us some of the most valuable truths we need for a lifetime of faithfulness.

A BETRAYAL (or, the danger of false repentance)

It was dark. They needed to arrest the right person. Judas would make sure of this. His signal would be a kiss. He approached with a large group of guards, sent from the religious leaders who wanted to rid themselves of Jesus, fearing the public's allegiance to Him and envious of the praise He had received. They would not take any chances. They came with swords, clubs, and a traitor. You have most likely heard the phrase *kiss of death*. Well, this is where it comes from. Judas's greeting of Jesus with a kiss on the cheek is unprecedented. And, as it turns out, treacherous.

Jesus says, "Have you come out as against a robber, with swords and clubs to capture me?" (Matt. 26:55). Apparently, the guards forgot who they were dealing with. The power that Jesus had shown in His public ministry did not come by the sword, so they wouldn't be able to stop Him with one. The disciples, however, didn't get it either. One of them draws his own sword. Blood is shed. The ear of one of the servants of the high priest is cut off. Whose hand is at the helm of this sword? We will get there in a moment, but Luke's gospel tells us that Jesus, in rebuke to such actions, heals the man's ear. If it seems as though Jesus has lost control, He removes all doubt when He says, "All this has taken place that the Scriptures ... might be fulfilled" (v. 56). Any attempt to deny or defend the mission of Jesus by force is doomed to failure.

Eventually, everyone will betray Jesus in some way or another, but why would Judas betray Him? It's fascinating to me that the only recorded dialogue between Judas and Jesus involves three things—a rebuke for his greed, his betrayal, and his unwillingness to admit it. Denial is a constant theme within the topic of temptation. Though we are not told of Judas's motives, the simplest answer for his betrayal is thirty pieces of silver, forever warning of the danger of following Jesus out of greed and self-service. He continually nursed his greed under the cover of being a disciple of Christ. (Another reason why it's so important to get to the heart!) What is it that he expected when it was all said and done? We don't know, but once Judas saw Jesus condemned later on, we are told that he changed his mind about the money.

At first glance, this may seem like a form of repentance. But why, then, does Judas's story end so tragically? The answer shows us the difference between true and false repentance. Because there are two ways to be lost. The first is to recognize what sin is and try to atone for it yourself. Once Judas experienced guilt for his sin, he refused to bring that burden of guilt to God; he refused to bring it to Christ. He carried it upon himself. And it drove him to his own death sentence. Recognizing sin is not enough; something must be done about our sin. But one thing is clear in Scripture—we cannot atone for it ourselves.

The second way to be lost is to pretend that your sin is not so bad or that it's nonexistent and therefore doesn't need to be dealt with. This was the case with the largest and loudest group in the crowd that night, the religious leaders.

AN ARREST (or, the blinding effect of pride)

Jesus was seized by the guards and taken to the house of the high priest where the rest of the leadership were waiting. The trial began, but everything about it was wrong. No trial, according to the law, was to be held at night. No capital verdict should have been reached in one day. Nor should the trial have taken place during Passover.

And the procedure for calling the witnesses was a disaster, full of misquotations and misrepresentations. But it didn't matter. They had already made up their minds. They were looking only for evidence that supported their preconceived verdict.

Pride is a powerful thing. Their pride blinded them to the truth. It's not that they could not see, but that they would not see. Such is always the case with pride. They were walking in darkness thinking that they were in the light. I cannot remember where I heard this, but I know I heard it the first week I was a new Christian: there are none so blind as those who choose not to see. Though they arrested Jesus and placed Him on trial, they were the ones on trial.

The only serious charge they could land against Jesus was, ironically, the one thing that was true: He claimed to be the Son of God. Impatient with Christ's patience during the trial, the high priest says, "I adjure you by the living God, tell us if you are the Christ, the Son of God" (Matt. 26:63). Christ responds, "You have said so. And in the future you will see Me vindicated" (author's paraphrase). This was all they needed. They condemned Him as being worthy of death for blasphemy. There was only one problem. The power to sentence one to death lay only with an official verdict from Rome, and that would have to wait until the morning. So the unofficial punishment began. They mocked Him, beat Him, spit on Him, and, one more terrible irony, blindfolded the only One who could truly help them see.

Why does Matthew record all of this for us? It's not only to un-cover the truth about our pride, but it's to prove the true identity of Jesus and show His faithfulness as a contrast to the failed religious lead-ership. Hundreds of years before, the prophet of the Old Testament foretold what God's rescuer of Israel and humanity would endure: that

He would be beaten, mocked, and scorned. All of this was told in advance. But why must it happen? Because the Savior must suffer in our place if we are to be saved from our sins. Without His sacrifice we would be left to bear this burden we could not carry, of a price we could not pay. In this trial, the most horrible things are happening and human evil is responsible. And yet as Jesus willingly surrenders Himself to it, He will bring about God's plan of salvation to deliver mankind from sin.

In the midst of all this madness, we are given one more vignette, one more story, and I think we are given it as both a warning and a hope. First, it shows us the progression of how we end up going down the road of denial and some of the lessons we have learned about temptation. But secondly, it show us how we can be delivered from denial and transformed through the process. It's the story of Peter's trial.

A DENIAL (or, the progression of compromise in temptation)

We are told that it was Peter's sword that chopped off the ear of the high priest's servant that night in the garden. Which is strange because Jesus had spoken again and again about the type of kingdom that He came to bring, that it would not be brought about by force or the sword. Peter knew this. But his instincts hadn't changed. He was stuck in old patterns, and when push came to shove, he went for the sword.

Many of us hear the truth of the gospel again and again. So much so that even the word *gospel* feels fatigued. And yet, in moments of testing, we fall back to the old patterns. The gospel may change our minds, but has it changed our instincts? The first step toward denial in the trial of Peter was acting out in self-confidence. Even attempting something in God's name, as Peter did on this night, must also be done in God's power and in God's ways. Jesus, graciously, cleans up the mess.

The next step toward denial for Peter was following at a distance. We are told that when Jesus was brought into the house of the high priest, Peter remained in the courtyard, incognito among the guards. Why? He wanted to see how it would end. It was his attempt to remain neutral and on the fence. This is an incredibly dangerous place to be because we mistake being a spectator for a disciple. Christ may be in the line of sight, but are we near? Are our hearts open to listen and receive correction? Or will we distance ourselves when the heat gets turned up? Are we afraid of being associated with Jesus when it gets controversial? People begin to question Peter. "Are you with that man, Jesus?" "No!" he says. There is a progression here with Peter in the narrative; with each conversation he moves farther and farther back, first to the courtyard, then to the fireside, and finally toward the exit. As it was with Peter, this fear of man acts like a gateway drug—you initially distance yourself, then move farther and farther away.

Why did Peter buckle under the pressure? After all, he was not in a courtroom bound by chains; he was in a courtyard standing beside ordinary people. A young girl asks, "Were you also with Jesus?" He gets defensive and responds, "I don't know what you mean!" Was it his desire to impress? This may be a particular weakness for us. We want so badly for people to think well of us that we compromise what is most important. Or could it have been indifference? Who cares about what a young girl thinks anyway? Well, according to Jesus, there are no insignificant people. And the mic is always on. And so begins Peter's train wreck. To a second woman he doubles his denial with an oath: "I

SWEAR I don't know Him!" And by the third conversation, he denies not only knowing Jesus but being one of His followers. Of course, this is quite easy for us to do, to distance ourselves from "other" Christians. The "Oh, I can't stand other Christians" approach is easy to take until we remember that Jesus died for their sins as well as ours. But Peter, not satisfied with an oath, goes on to a curse: "May God destroy me if I am lying. I don't know the man!"

And then the rooster crowed. And Peter wept.

Whether it's through valiant acts of self-confidence or through embarrassed escapes, this story of swords and shadows represents the very things we resort to in order to save ourselves in moments of temptation. In the story of Judas, the religious leaders, and Peter, we have a picture of human weakness. Of our weakness. Though our particular temptations may look a little different, we are all responsible for how we face our trials. Whether through attack or abandonment, behind the back or to the face, whether with a kiss or a fist, all of us have gone astray.

And yet, though there are one thousand different ways we can turn from Jesus, we all share the same way back. It's through His faithfulness.

A RETURN (or, the beauty of mercy in our moment of need)

How would it feel to lock eyes with Jesus when you have just denied Him? That night, across the courtyard, in Peter's moment of denial, Jesus looked at Peter. What was the look that Jesus gave? Was it a look of disgust? Was it a look of "typical Peter …"? No. I believe it was the look of mercy.

Luke's gospel tells us what it was that Peter remembered. Before the trial Jesus said to Peter, "Satan demanded to have you, that he might sift you like wheat, but I have prayed for you that your faith may not fail. And when you have turned again, strengthen your brothers" (22:31–32). Here we find the source of our hope in trial, that Jesus has stood in our place and on our behalf. How can He look upon Peter, and me and you, with mercy in the moment of failure? Because He went under the sword of judgment and into the shadow of darkness when He went to the cross. There, Jesus went through the trial and judgment that our sins deserve so that we might get the verdict His innocence deserves. Jesus did not endure the trial of His last night because He was bound by chains; He did so because He was bound by love. He stood firm under fire. It's in looking to Him, knowing that He has stood in our place and prayed for us, that restores us and keeps our faith from failing.

Peter's repentance is presented in contrast to Judas's pseudo-repentance. When Judas saw his sin, he turned to himself to pay the cost; when Peter saw his sin, he turned to Christ who paid the cost. John Calvin, in commenting on this passage, says, "The example teaches us that however lame our repentance, yet we may have a good hope. As long as it is sincere, God scorns not even feeble repentance."[2] True repentance is not about "doing enough" in our own strength. True repentance is about seeing our sin for what it is and then seeing our Savior for who He is. Though we mourn our unfaithfulness, we rejoice in Christ's faithfulness. Only this will heal a shattered heart and cleanse a guilty conscience. Through faith, not works, we are made right before God and robed in the righteousness of Jesus.

THE TRUTH ABOUT HUMAN WEAKNESS

It would be foolish for me to read about Judas, the religious leaders, or even Peter and think that their temptations would never tempt me. How often do I attempt a valiant act of good and yet operate out of self-confidence? Or insist that I am right, even when the facts prove otherwise? Or shrink back out of fear over other people's perceptions? These are temptations for us all. "Let anyone who thinks that he stands take heed lest he fall" (1 Cor. 10:12).

I'm sure we all have stories like Peter's. When I was a new Christian, perhaps just a few months into my faith, an old friend approached me about what I believed. I didn't tell him. I was even pressed with questions such as, "What is there to believe about God?" or "How is it that we know where to find peace in life?" But frankly, I was afraid of being ridiculed for my beliefs and was enjoying our times of mindless fun too much, so I would quickly change the subject. It wasn't long before I fell back into my old patterns with my old friend. One by one, the old habits started creeping back in, but I was blind to the progression because I wasn't willing to admit that anything had changed. I was having a good time. But in reality I was moving back into the shadows. A few months prior, I was like Peter before the trial, bold and passionate. But I soon realized that without relying on Jesus's upholding strength, I can get knocked over by the smallest thing. We need to be honest about human weakness.

Wait a minute, won't this keep me from stepping out at all? Moving forward in my life? No. Awareness of human weakness should not keep us from stepping out boldly; it should keep us from stepping out boldly *without God*. We would be wrong to think that God would never restore fallen people. Look at Peter! One moment a failure, the next moment a powerful leader in a new movement that would change history. But it was not because he was unaware of his weakness; it was because in his weakness he learned to look upon Christ.

When the gospel goes down deep, it changes not only your mind but also your patterns and your instincts. No more swords, no more shadows. It's as we become aware of our weaknesses that we learn to let go of the sword and clasp our hands in prayer, and we see the power of God work through us. It's through this humble brokenness that we become changed men and women. Who would you rather be with? A friend who is unaware of his or her weaknesses and unwilling to admit them or someone who is gladly willing to open up and admit the struggle and depend on the grace of God for help? Commentator Dale Bruner says that "an unbroken Peter would have been an unbearable Peter."[3] It's true, we learn the gospel best when we need it the most. If there is hope for Peter, then there is hope for me and you.

THE TRUTH OF CHRIST'S FAITHFULNESS

Our failures need not define us. In this whole story we are given a picture of a great denial, and yet through repentance there is great restoration! The first truth convicts us; the second truth comforts us. Jesus warns us from presumption and rescues us from condemnation. It's in turning to Christ that we experience both.

After the "relapse" in my native Bay Area, I moved to Southern California to enroll in Bible school. Several weeks in, I came under the strong conviction concerning my dishonesty with my old friend.

He had real questions and real struggles, and yet I buckled under my own insecurity. I assumed that he would simply laugh off my faith and disregard me altogether. But as I was being brought to my senses, I experienced the freedom of getting over myself as the Holy Spirit brought the truth of Christ to bear on my heart. I was compelled. I had to call up my friend and share the truth. "I haven't been honest with you about my life and what I believe," I said when I called from a pay phone (remember those?). "I believe that God sent His Son, Jesus, into our world to rescue us from sin." Silence. I thought, *Oh no, he thinks this is absurd.* But then I heard tears. "Can I be saved?" was the question that came on the other end of the line. That day I was able to lead that friend to Christ and watch him experience the joy of finding eternal life.

Now I know it doesn't always turn out that way—old friends being converted—but I learned two simple lessons that day. One, that God is gracious. He was so patient with me, leading me away from my fear of man. And two, Jesus really is what people need. May Christ give us the confidence that we need to bear witness to Him in every aspect of our lives. And when we fall, we can simply turn back to Him in repentance and watch His wonderful work of restoration.

This trial gives us a picture of both human weakness and divine faithfulness. It's given to us so that none of us presume and that all of us have hope, remembering the good news to be this—the faithfulness of Jesus is greater than the failure of man. Through faith in Christ you don't lead a life *for* a verdict; you lead your life *from* a verdict—justified. This is the hope in our trial.

chapter ten

THIS IS YOUR LEGACY

Now therefore in the sight of all Israel, the assembly of the LORD, and in
the hearing of our God, observe and seek out all the commandments
of the LORD your God, that you may possess this good land and
leave it for an inheritance to your children after you forever.
"And you, Solomon my son, know the God of your father and
serve him with a whole heart and with a willing mind."
1 Chronicles 28:8–9

This past summer I took my family to the beautiful San Francisco Bay Area for a vacation. Other than personal ministry trips over the years, I had never taken my whole family to visit, and I was really excited to show them where I grew up. Among all the fun things I had planned, I knew there would also be a more somber moment. I hadn't visited the place my father was buried since the week he passed, and I knew I wanted to take my kids there. My father died long before any of my kids were born, so it was an opportunity to reflect on my side of the family and tell them stories about the grandpa they had not gotten to meet. On the day we visited, as I was remembering all the things my father had passed down to me before he died, I began to think deeply about what I would leave to my children, what I would pass on to them. I am only thirty-five, but we all know that life is a vapor and tomorrow is promised to no man. Am I living my life now in such a way that it impacts my children for the kingdom of God? That question is now on my mind constantly.

If you had only a month left to live, what would you absolutely need to pass on to family and friends? What would you be leaving them with? I'm not just thinking of material things or property, though these things can be great to pass on. I am talking about the whole of your life, the lessons learned, your legacy. What would you say is so important that you would just have to communicate it in the final weeks of your life? It's an important question because, whether you are prepared or not, you are leaving something right now, an example and impression. This is part of your legacy. We are each building one through the choices we make. The temptation is to think that it doesn't matter.

A great lie that has caught many hearts is the lie that your life and character don't matter. It's a lie that consumes some even to the point of lethargy, depression, or even self-destructive thoughts. The truth could not be more opposite. Your life is not only precious because it was created by God, but it also counts for the effect and influence it has on others. The type of person you become over the years impacts family, friends, coworkers, neighbors, and people that you may even have no idea about. Overcoming sin and temptation should not only be thought of in terms of individual health and growth but also in relation to community. The person I am becoming right now reverberates to the lives of my wife and kids, my church and neighbors, and people I may not even know. What will my legacy be? What should it be?

I have spoken a lot about choices—how your choices shape your character, and your character in turn shapes what you become. The poet Emerson famously put it like this: "Sow a thought and you reap an action; sow an act and you reap a habit; sow a habit and you reap a character; sow a character and you reap a destiny." When you think of influence and legacy, don't just think about the end of your life; think about what you are doing now, your time at home, in the school, on the job, away on travel. Think about your church, the involvement you have, and how you are currently using your gifts. All these things are a part of your character.

The life of David, as I have pointed out earlier, is studied time and again by many—not only because the Bible gives an incredible amount of space to his life, but also because in studying his life, we are observing how and why he becomes a man after God's own heart. At the very end of his life, he gives a moving speech to his son Solomon in front of the gathered leaders of Israel. In it, he passes the torch to his son who will rule in his place, and as he does, he also shares a lifetime of lessons. He is essentially saying, "Here is what is important…" "Here is the work you must do…" "Here is the example I have for you…" "Here are the lessons I have learned…." These words, though spoken by King David to his son Solomon, are in some ways spoken to us today. They contain truth for every heart and lessons for every life, and you don't need to wait till your deathbed to hear them. What are we given in David's last words about temptation, and who will we become?

A PATTERN IN LIFE

If you followed me around for several weeks in a row, which is a slightly awkward thought, I wonder what you would discover about my habits and patterns. How I spend my time, money, and energy. It's something I think about often, because it makes me realize that I am, even right now, forming patterns that affect not only my soul but also the souls around me. I want to live my life in such a way that I set a pattern that others can follow.

I will admit, when I first read the apostle Paul's words on this topic, I was taken aback. He says in his letter to the Philippian church: "Join in imitating me" (3:17). Is Paul a self-centered narcissist? But then I realized what the rest of the verse makes clear. He wasn't asking people to focus on him per se, but to join him in dependence on God. Making this crystal clear, he writes, "Keep your eyes on those who walk according to the example you have in us." From an Old Testament perspective, we can learn a similar lesson from David. Like him, we often fail, and we give in to the temptations of the world, the flesh, and the Devil. David failed too. However, he recognized that about himself and didn't try to whitewash his past mistakes. And in this he leaves us a pattern to follow.

The first thing that stands out about David's pattern in life is that it's honest. The worst thing we could do is pretend that we don't struggle with temptation or cover up that we have given in. As we have already learned, to choose that path is just to give in to another kind of temptation. Instead, David openly acknowledges his past. Yes, he had done great things, but he was also a man of blood—he had committed adultery and was guilty of murder. But he also knew that he was forgiven by God, as all of us can be. The lesson I see in David about who we will become is that it destroys common misperceptions about our growth. We often imagine our maturing process as a straight trend line on a chart going up. That is the perception. But the reality is different. In reality, maturity looks more like our financial charts, with spikes and drops along the way. So, in admitting his failures, David actually sets a pattern for us—one of honesty and repentance. It must be part of our daily life in the battle against sin and temptation. Each time we move in this direction, we grow in the truth.

One of the hardest things to do as a parent is confess your sin to your children. The other night I was praying with my seven-year-old before bed when I confessed sin in my prayers. My daughter stopped me in the middle and said, "Daddy, you don't sin, do you?" Think about all the ways I could have capitalized on this! It would have been so easy to say, "Well, honey, Daddy really is that awesome and he never sins!" But as you can guess, I didn't say that. But that didn't make it easy to acknowledge to her the different ways I also give in to temptation. Hopefully, I am setting a pattern she can follow.

The second thing that stands out about David's speech at the end is that it was humble. In the chapter quoted earlier (1 Chron. 28), there is this grand scene where all the leaders of Israel are gathered together waiting for the great king to give them instruction and vision for the future. Yet, though he is a king, Israel's greatest, he refers to his countrymen and servants as "brethren." Because although David knew his position was great, it was itself a gift of God. This reflects one of the great virtues that every follower of Jesus should cultivate and give attention to: humility. It comes by seeing ourselves in light of who God is. Every good thing we have in our lives is not deserved; it's given by the kindness of our God. Remember in the wilderness? This is how Satan tried to tempt Jesus, to get Him, and us, to separate the gift from the Giver. If we make this connection day by day, understanding that God's grace is the reason for the very breath in our lungs, it will produce humility. And humility is one of the greatest legacies you could leave. Why? Because it points us to God instead of ourselves.

As evangelicals, we have mastered the deceptive art of false humility. We are, for the most part, too savvy for our own good. We grow up watching people publicly deflect praise but privately storing and nurturing it in their own hearts. David's life and David's repentance offer a blueprint for humility and a stunning contrast to the kind of image-driven false humility we see so often.

Lastly, David's pattern in life is practical. He stored up resources so that the people after him could get to work and build for God's kingdom. As Christians, we are called to invest our time, talent, and treasure together into the life of the church and the mission of God. In fact, as we do, we will not be as prone to give in to the temptation to use all our resources for selfish gain. Could the people close to you follow the example of how you invest in your community? Or would they conclude that you are indifferent? These are good questions to ask. But why does it all matter?

A PURPOSE FOR LIFE

We are told from the youngest age that we should find a purpose in life, as if purpose is sold at Target and we just have to pick the one we like and bring it to the checkout stand. Don't misunderstand me, we *need* purpose! Without it we fall into despair! But my point is that when, for example, David in his final speech talks about the mission of life, he does not give a generic purpose; he gives us *the* purpose. And it's set out for us by David in three simple phrases he gives to his son: know God, serve God, and seek God.

David says to his son, "You want to be a good king? Have a real relationship with God." The phrase "to know" is a powerful term that speaks of intimacy and nearness. It doesn't just mean you have information about it, but that you set your affections on it. We do this all the time with lesser things. For example, our careers. If you want to succeed in a particular field, say finance, you don't just study for it; you dream about it. It can quickly become the center of your life. But if anything other than God is the center and focus, then your whole life will revolve around something that can never sustain it.

Again, we're not immune to this in the church. We encourage our talented young men in their careers because, at some level, we love money and we love associating with successful people. However, like David, perhaps we need to be challenging one another to have real relationships with God.

It's interesting to me that David shares this piece of advice with his son, who has grown up his whole life hearing about God. Is that redundant? No. David is saying, "Solomon, know the God we are always talking about! Open up your heart to Him! Set your affections on Him!" This is how we are to understand purpose in life. It means, practically, that you are a child of God first, and a _____ (fill in the blank with your career) second. For me this means I am a child of God first and a husband/father/friend/pastor after that. If we reverse this, then God is dishonored and we suffer. We turn lesser things into idols that will break our hearts. Know Him. This is life.

What is the evidence of knowing God? How would others know that we know God? By serving God. Putting into practice what we know honors Him and lines up with how He has told us to live. The character that we develop in the process of serving God acts like a microphone for our words.

We must not only speak the truth but live it out as well. The two go hand in hand. Serving God is the evidence of knowing God. Here is what happens when we leave out one or the other. If we only serve God but don't know God, we are just trying to follow rules but without a relationship and therefore without the power of new affections. On the other hand, if we just claim to know but not serve, then we are disobeying and disregarding everything He has called us to do. Both are tragic mistakes. Serving God without knowing God is slavery. Knowing God without serving Him is disloyalty. But knowing God and serving Him is love.

The very fruit of our relationship with God is evidenced in our character, which is why character matters so much. Satan knows this, so he will therefore design his temptations and lies to split the relationship between you and your God. Overcoming this means staying as close to God as possible. But David also addresses the motive with which we do. He says, "Serve God with a whole heart." This does not mean a perfect heart. If that were the case, we are all doomed. No, it means a devoted heart. It means you don't chop up parts of your life and give God a portion. We must recognize that the whole of life must be connected to God.

To move forward in the way God would have us means to know, serve, and, lastly, seek God all our days. This is about commitment. You don't have to wait until the end of your life to seek God, nor is this an attribute of certain types of special Christians. This is for everyone, young and old, rich and poor … We are to seek God. As we do, He will be found. He is not playing some kind of cruel game of hide-and-seek. He has revealed Himself ultimately in Jesus. Every soul is lost because of sin, but the good news is that God sent His Son to seek and save those who are lost. He opened the way! We can seek Him because He has sought us. We seek God by believing, and continuing to believe in Jesus. There will never be a person in the universe who will be able to say, "I sought for mercy in Jesus, but I didn't find it." The Bible says if you want mercy, you will find it, if you seek God! If you ask for salvation, you will have it. As Jesus said, "Whoever comes to me I will never cast out" (John 6:37). But what if we are too far gone? Is there hope?

I want everyone to be perfectly clear on this. If you trust your soul to Jesus, you are saved. No one is too guilty or too good. No one is too guilty that he or she can't be saved, and no one is too good that he or she doesn't need to be saved. We all ought to seek God and we all can seek God, by trusting and following Jesus. This is the purpose, but we are not only left there.

A PROMISE FOR LIFE

The end of this final speech echoes many other passing-the-torch speeches in the Bible, such as Moses giving a charge to Joshua or the apostle Paul charging Timothy. But before we think about what the promise in the speech means for us, we need to put ourselves for a moment in David's shoes so that we can begin to see the important role we all have in passing on truth to others so that they can overcome the lies that would keep them from life. Because we are all links in a chain, both giving and receiving truth that we might walk in victory. What a shame it would be if David did not pass on an example to Solomon, and what a shame it would be if Solomon did not receive it!

This final charge from David's speech actually ends with a promise, and this promise is actually also given to everyone who believes. In verse 20 of 1 Chronicles 28, he says, "Then David said to Solomon his son, 'Be strong and courageous and do it. Do not be afraid and do not be dismayed, for the LORD God, even my God, is with you. He will not leave you or forsake you, until all the work for the service of the house of the LORD is finished.'" By the power of the Holy Spirit, God is with us! He will not leave us nor forsake us! So ... that means we can get to work. Work together. And finish the work. That is what I was thinking about when I saw my father's grave, and it's what I think about when I hear David's last words.

Have you ever wondered what will be written on your tombstone? I don't want to be morbid or anything, but if your life were summarized in a short and concise way, what would it say? I think that one of the greatest and simplest eulogies in the Bible is actually about David. When Peter the apostle is preaching a sermon in the book of Acts, he references King David, and when he does, he simply says this: "For David, after he had served the purpose of God in his own generation, fell asleep and was laid with his fathers" (Acts 13:36). Basically, "This guy served God, then died."

Now that is a great eulogy.

When I was a young Christian, I started reading church history and learning about various movements and leaders who had made an impact. One person who has always stood out is a powerful preacher named George Whitefield. In the period of the Great Awakening, the guy preached his face off, riding horseback from town to town and preaching outdoors to crowds upward of thousands, all without modern amplification. Toward the end of his life, his health started to decline, but this did not keep him from publicly addressing the masses. In 1770, the fifty-five-year-old continued his preaching tour despite his declining health. He preached long and powerfully as he stood atop a barrel, crying out in tones of thunder about the truths of the gospel. When he was finished, he went home, lit a candle, went upstairs, and entered into glory.

That is amazing.

The reason it's vital for us to understand this topic of temptation is because giving in to it will rob us of what matters most. God allows it into our lives as an opportunity for us to cling more closely to Him and His purposes for our lives. As we do, we grow powerfully, and it's not because of what is in us but because of what is in Him. Every moment that we do this, we are flexing that spiritual muscle and becoming the types of people who will point others to Jesus. And that is what we are to give our lives to.

I don't want to get to the end of my days and say, "I stood on the sidelines and critiqued how everyone else served God or didn't serve God in their generation." Do you? For those of you who are older, are you passing down what you have learned? Are you teaching those younger than yourself the insight you have gained through your defeats and victories? Or are you just complaining about their immaturity?

For those who are younger, are you teachable? Or do you think you have it all figured out? Let us just humble ourselves and recognize that we all have something to learn and we all have something to teach. David, though imperfect and flawed, devoted his son Solomon to God and educated him to know God. A great example.

The legacy we leave is the person we become. That is why the choices we make now matter. And that is why we must fight the temptation to give in or give up. We are all far from perfect, but I don't want to just maintain. We are called to work together to push back the kingdom of darkness and see lives made new by the power of the gospel.

You have this incredible relationship with God through Christ; don't give it up. You have, as a result, an incredible purpose; give yourself to it. Even in the smallest of daily decisions. And when you are done, God will take you home and you will be glorified.

Solomon, unfortunately, began well but did not finish well. Like many of the kings of Israel, he was flawed. At their best they can point us to God. But Jesus, the perfect King, came and did what neither David nor Solomon nor we could do: bring us to God. He did so by laying down His life, not just for His generation but for the whole world. Because of the sacrifice and resurrection of Jesus, we can be sure of the promises of God and be confident that He can fulfill His purposes through us. Let's lay hold of this.

If you know the King and follow Him through the wilderness and through the temptations of life, building on the truth and not the lie, your legacy will not be perfection … but it will point others to grace.

My prayer is that the impression we leave, the influence we impart, and the legacy we leave would simply point people to Jesus. After all, He is what the world needs and what matters most. And when temptation comes, you and I have the privilege of showing it.

NOTES

Chapter 1: The Trouble with Temptation

1. Associated Press, "South Korea Ferry Passengers Recall Moments of Bravery from Crew," *The Guardian*, April 22, 2014, www.theguardian.com/world /2014/apr/22/south-korea-ferry-disaster-passengers-bravery-crew.
2. N. T. Wright's book *After You Believe: Why Christian Character Matters* (New York: HarperCollins, 2010) is a wonderful resource on Christian virtue.
3. C. S. Lewis, *Mere Christianity* (New York: HarperCollins, 2009), 71.
4. Alain de Botton, *The Consolations of Philosophy* (New York: Vintage International, 2013), Kindle edition, 7.

Chapter 2: An Education in Grace

1. Perhaps the most famous and formative sermon on this theme is "The Expulsive Power of a New Affection" by Thomas Chalmers. Google it.
2. "List of religions and spiritual traditions," *Wikipedia*, http://en.wikipedia.org/wiki /List_of_religions_and_spiritual_traditions.

Chapter 3: Who You Will Become

1. C. S. Lewis, *Mere Christianity* (New York: HarperCollins, 2009), 121–22.
2. John Owen, *Overcoming Sin and Temptation*, ed. Kelly M. Kapic and Justin Taylor (Wheaton, IL: Crossway, 2006), 152.

Chapter 4: When Independence Lies

1. Henri J. Nouwen, *A Spirituality of Living* (Nashville, TN: Upper Room, 2011), 12.

Chapter 5: A Habitat for Divinity

1. Trevin Wax, "Worth a Look," *Kingdom People*, March 4, 2015, The Gospel Coalition, www.thegospelcoalition.org/blogs/trevinwax/2015/03/04/worth -a-look-3-4-15/.

2. "Heaven Less Opulent Than Vatican, Reports Disappointed Pope," *The Onion*, April 13, 2005, www.theonion.com/articles/heaven-less-opulent-than-vatican -reports-disappoin-1315.

3. Warren W. Wiersbe, *The Strategy of Satan: How to Detect and Defeat Him* (Carol Stream, IL: Tyndale, 1979), x.

Chapter 6: When Religion Lies

1. Christopher Hitchens, *God Is Not Great: How Religion Poisons Everything* (New York: Twelve, 2007).

2. Ross Douthat, *Bad Religion: How We Became a Nation of Heretics* (New York: Free Press, 2012), 3.

3. Henri J. Nouwen, *In the Name of Jesus: Reflections on Christian Leadership* (New York: Crossroad, 1990), 59.

4. I remember the famous Holocaust survivor Corrie ten Boom used an illustration like this, and it has always stuck with me.

Chapter 7: The Art of Killing Sin

1. Jeré Longman, "Blurry Target Is No Trouble for Ace Archer," *New York Times*, July 28, 2012, www.nytimes.com/2012/07/29/sports/olympics/with-impaired -vision-blurry-target-is-no-trouble-for-south-korean-archer.html?_r=0.

2. John Owen, *Overcoming Sin and Temptation*, ed. Kelly M. Kapic and Justin Taylor (Wheaton, IL: Crossway, 2006), 74.

3. Owen, *Overcoming Sin*, 88.

4. Owen, *Overcoming Sin*, 99.

Chapter 8: When Success Lies

1. George Mallory in 1922, www.mnteverest.net/quote.html.

2. David Breashears and Audrey Salkeld, *Last Climb: The Legendary Everest Expeditions of George Mallory* (Washington, DC: National Geographic, 1999), 17.

3. Zack Eswine, *Sensing Jesus: Life and Ministry as a Human Being* (Wheaton, IL: Crossway, 2012), 64.

4. Alain de Botton, *Status Anxiety* (New York: Vintage, 2005), 175.

5. Louise Story, "Anywhere the Eye Can See, It's Likely to See an Ad," *New York Times*, January 15, 2007, www.nytimes.com/2007/01/15/business/media/15everywhere.html?.

6. Dietrich Bonhoeffer, *Creation and Fall / Temptation: Two Biblical Studies* (New York: Touchstone, 1997), 132.

7. C. S. Lewis, *The Weight of Glory* (New York: HarperCollins, 2001), 32.

Chapter 9: The Hope in Our Trial

1. Polly Curtis, "Gordon Brown Calls Labour Supporter a 'Bigoted Woman,'" *The Guardian*, April 28, 2010, www.theguardian.com/politics/2010/apr/28/gordon-brown-bigoted-woman.

2. *Calvin's New Testament Commentaries: A Harmony of the Gospels—Matthew, Mark, and Luke, and the Epistles of James and Jude* (Grand Rapids, MI: Eerdmans, 1995), 173.

3. Frederick Dale Bruner, *Matthew: A Commentary: The Churchbook, Matthew 13–28* (Grand Rapids, MI: Eerdmans, 2004), 700.